PEOPLE, WORK AND DEVELOPMENT

HEINEMANN GEOGRAPHY *for* **AVERY HILL**

Gary Cambers • *Stuart Currie*

Heinemann Educational Publishers
Halley Court, Jordan Hill, Oxford, OX2 8EJ
a division of Reed Educational & Professional Publishing Ltd
Heinemann is a registered trademark of Reed Educational & Professional Publishing Ltd

OXFORD MELBOURNE AUCKLAND
JOHANNESBURG BLANTYRE GABORONE
IBADAN PORTSMOUTH NH (USA) CHICAGO

Text © Gary Cambers, Stuart Currie

First edition published 1999
Second edition published 2001

ISBN 0 435 35406X

05 04 03 02 01
10 9 8 7 6 5 4 3 2 1

Designed and typeset by The Wooden Ark, Leeds
Printed and bound in Spain by Edelvives

Acknowledgements
The authors and publishers would like to thank the following for permission to reproduce copyright material.

Maps and extracts
p. 7B Farmers' Weekly 6.12.2001; **p. 7B** reproduced by kind permission of the Leicester Mercury; **p. 8D** Maps reproduced from Ordnance Survey mapping with the permission of the Controller of Her Majesty's Stationary Office, © Crown copyright, License no. 10000230; **p. 9F** The Times 28 September 2000 and 28 March 2001; **p. 11E and F** UNESCO; **p. 11G** Financial Times 6 November 1996; **p. 12B** Financial Times 1 December 1998; **p. 12B** Press Trust of India; **p. 13F** Down to Earth volume 9; **p. 17E** Matthew Parris, Inca Kola, Orion Books Ltd; **p. 18C** Richard Howard, Black Cargo; **p. 57** Wayland Publishers Ltd; **p. 21E** The Sunday Times 13 March 1998; **p. 22B** Eurostat, The World: A Third World Guide; **p. 23C** The Sunday Times 10 December 2000; **p. 23E** The Sunday Times 13 March 1998; **p. 24A** The Brandt Report, 1980 Pan Publications; **p. 26B** The Human Development Report 1997; **p. 26C, p. 27D** The Human Development Report 2000; **p. 27E** Concern Worldwide, 248-250 Lavender Hill, London, SW11 1LJ; **p. 28A** Human Development Report 1995 and 1997; **p. 28A** World's Women 2000; **p. 28A** World Development Indicators, 1997; **p. 29F** UNDP Choices, October 1997; **p. 30B** Financial Times 24 June 1997; **p. 31D** Amnesty International; **p. 31E** Anti-slavery International leaflet; **p. 33D** World Development Movement; **p. 34B** The Times 10 August 1995; **p. 35C** Cafédirect; **p. 38A, 39E, 40A** Maps reproduced from Ordnance Survey mapping with the permission of the Controller of Her Majesty's Stationary Office, © Crown copyright, License no. 10000230; **p. 42A** World Report on Azerbaijan; **p. 43D** Financial Times 3 March 1998; **p.43D** Oil and Gas Journal 2000; **p. 43E** The Times 5 May 1998; **p. 44B** Invest in Britain Bureau; **p. 44C and D, Sunday Times 5 May 1998, 4 June 1996; **p. 45F and G** Financial Times 3 November 1999, 5 November 1997; **p. 46A** The Times 11 July 1996; **p. 46B** Maps reproduced from Ordnance Survey mapping with the permission of the Controller of Her Majesty's Stationary Office, © Crown copyright, License no. 10000230; **p. 47C and D** LG Project News, Lucky Goldstar, September 1997; **p. 49D** Financial Times 18 February 1997; **p. 52B** Maps reproduced from Ordnance Survey mapping with the permission of the Controller of Her Majesty's Stationary Office, © Crown copyright, License no. 10000230; The Independent on Sunday 14 March 1993; p. 54B The Ruhr District Studies on a German Region; **p. 55D** The Guardian 13 March 1993; **p. 56** IBA Emscher Booklet; **p. 58C** Maps reproduced from Ordnance Survey mapping with the permission of the Controller of Her Majesty's Stationary Office, © Crown copyright, License no. 10000230; **p. 59G** The Times 27 April 2001; **p. 61**C Madeline Ashcroft, The Guardian; **p. 61C** Tourism Concern.

Photographs
The cover photograph shows ship repair workers in Singapore; Hutchison Library.
p. 5, Network/Sebastiao Salgado; **p. 6** (Fig A1) Tony Stone Images; **p. 6** (Fig A2) Panos Pictures; **p. 6** (Fig A3) Bubbles/Jennie Woodcock; **p. 6** (Fig A4) Network; **p. 6** (Fig A5) Panos PicturesDaniel O'Leary; **p. 6** (Fig A6) Tony Stone Images; **p. 6** (Fig A7) Robert Harding; **p. 7** Associated Press; **p. 8** (Fig A) Popperfoto; **p. 8** (Fig B) Collections; **p. 9** (Fig G) Collections/Brian Sheull; **p. 9** (Fig H) Collections/Geoff Howard; **p. 10** (Fig A) Still Pictures; **p. 10** (Fig B) Tony Stone Images; **p. 10** (Fig C) Still Pictures; **p. 11** Financial Times; **p. 13** Rex Features; **p. 14** National office of statistics; **p. 15** Associated Press; **p. 16** (Fig A1) Gary Cambers; **p. 16** (Fig A2) Collections; **p. 16** (Fig A3) Collections; **p. 17** (Fig E1) Orion Books Ltd.; **p. 17** (Fig E2) Still Pictures; **p. 17** (Fig E3) Still Pictures; **p. 18** Mary Evans Picture; **p. 19** (Fig D1) Popperfoto; **p. 19** (Fig D2) Robert Harding; *p. 20* (Fig A1) Topham Picturepoint; **p. 20** (Fig A2) Topham Picturepoint; **p. 20** (Fig A3) Popperfoto; **p. 21** (Fig E1) Popperfoto; **p. 21** (Fig E2) Robert Harding; **p. 21** (Fig E3) Gary Cambers; **p. 21** (Fig E4) Gary Cambers; **p. 21** (Fig E5) Popperfoto/Reuters; **p. 23** Alistair Miller; **p. 25** Panos Pictures/Jeremy Horner; **p. 26** (Fig A1) Still Pictures; **p. 26** (Fig A2) Network/Homer Skyes; **p. 26** (Fig A3) Panos Pictures; **p. 26** (Fig A4) Network/K. Brimacombe; **p. 27** (Fig E) Still Pictures; **p. 27** (Fig F1) Stock Market; **p. 27** (Fig F2) Collections; **p. 27** (Fig F3) Panos Pictures; **p. 27** (Fig F4) Panos Pictures; **p. 27** (Fig F5) Mike Rideout; **p. 29** (Fig B) NUNDP/Jorgen Schytte; **p. 29** (Fig E) UNDP; **p. 30** Still Pictures/Rajendra Shaw/Christian Aid; p.31 (Fig D) Still Pictures; **p. 31** (Fig E) Rugmark logo; **p. 32** (Fig A1) Still Pictures/Reinhard Janke; **p. 32** (Fig A2) Robert Harding; **p. 33** (Fig E) Panos Pictures/Clive Shirley; **p. 33** (Fig F2) Oxfam/Sarah Errington; **p. 34** (Fig B1) News International; **p. 34** (Fig B2) BBC; **p. 35** (Fig C1) Body Shop; **p. 35** (Fig C2) Roger Scruton; **p. 35** (Fig C4) Co-op; **p. 36** UNDP; **p. 37** Silicon Maps Inc; **p. 38** (Fig B) Alyson Currie; **p. 38** (Fig C) Alyson Currie; **p. 38** (Fig D) Alyson Currie; **p. 39** Alyson Currie; **p. 42** (Fig A) Panos Pictures; **p. 42** (Fig C) Tacis News; **p. 46** Hugh Evans; **p. 47** Lucky Goldstar; **p. 48** (Fig A) Popperfoto; **p. 48** (Fig B) Popperfoto; **p. 48** (Fig D) Singapore Tourist Office; **p. 49** (Fig E1) Panos Pictures; **p. 50** (Fig A) Robert Harding; **p. 50** (Fig C) CGU; **p. 51** (Fig E1) TRIP; **p. 51** (Fig E2) Robert Harding; **p. 52** Dirft; **p. 53** Corbis; **p. 54** Rex Features; **p. 55** Article from the Guardian; **p. 56** (top) Emscher Park; **p. 56** (bottom left) Emscher Park; **p. 56** (bottom right) Emscher Park; **p. 57** (top) Emscher Park; **p. 57** (bottom) Emscher Park; **p. 58** (Fig A) Rex Features; **p. 58** (Fig B) Rex Features; **p. 59** Thomas Cooke; **p. 60** (Fig A1) Still Pictures/Chris Caldicott; **p. 60** (Fig A2) Still Pictures/Chris Caldicott; **p. 60** (Fig A3) Robert Harding/Robert Harris; **p. 61** (Fig B) Associated Press/John McConnico; **p. 61** (Fig C) Panos Pictures/Chris Stowers.

The publishers have made every effort to trace the copyright holders, but if they have inadvertently overlooked any, they will be pleased to make the necessary arrangements at the first opportunity.

Contents

Location of case studies

1 Employment structures and patterns

- **1** UK
- **2** India

2 Development, trade and aid

- **1** Peru
- **2** Ghana
- **3** Sierra Leone
- **4** EU
- **5** Argentina
- **6** India
- **7** Mali

3 Economic activity

- **1** UK – Northhamptonshire, Nottinghamshire, and Linconshire
- **2** Azerbaijan
- **3** Wales – Newport
- **4** Singapore

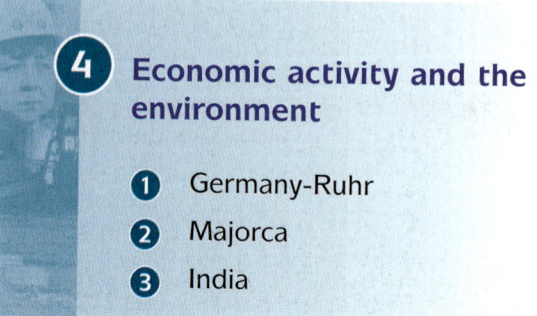

4 Economic activity and the environment

- **1** Germany-Ruhr
- **2** Majorca
- **3** India

1

Employment structures and patterns

KEY IDEAS

Employment structures vary in time and space.

Variations in employment structures and opportunities affect people.

Employment structures and patterns may change in future

Thirty thousand Brazilians dig for gold at the Sorra Pelada mine

1.1 Work and employment

What is employment?
What are the differences between formal and informal work?
Why do employment opportunities change with time?

A *Different people – different work*

Assembling televisions

Growing mange tout in Guatemala

Locksmith in Gujarat, India

Washing-up at home

Selling The Big Issue, London

Telemarketing

College students

1 a Describe the work shown in each photo in **Source A**.
b Suggest which of the forms of work are paid and which are unpaid.
c Explain why people do unpaid work.

2 a Make a list of the work done by members of your own family.
b Divide this into paid and unpaid work.
c Compare the work *you* do each day with that of other members of your group.

HERDSPERSON

Second in charge on four-person team. 400+ FH cows on all new unit. Rotary parlour, mattressed cubicles, long grazing season. Dairy/young stock experience essential. DIY A1 (training available). Excellent remuneration includes good centrally heated house with oil rayburn on farm in attractive coastal location. Regular time off (5½ day week if required). Company pension scheme.

Tel: 01437 781219 or write to:
F Hiam Ltd, Lower Broadmoor, Talbenny, Haverfordwest, Pembrokeshire, SA62 3XD

FLUTTERS BINGO CLUB
HINCKLEY

Require a
FULL TIME ASSISTANT MANAGER

Maturity and some experience beneficial. Evenings weeks/weekend hours. Salary £10–£12,000 per annum plus possible accommodation.

**ALSO:
PART TIME
OFFICE CLERK**
2-3 mornings

PREMIER PATTERN MAKING CO. Ltd.
79 Coleman Road Leicester, LE5 4LE
Tel: (0116) 276 6094

THIS YEARS SCHOOL LEAVERS 16–18 YR OLDS – INTERESTED IN CARPENTRY AND JOINERY

We are offereing a full apprenticeship for enthusiastic young people. Tools allowance. Reasonable wages. To manufacture timber moulds for the concrete industry. The position offers varied and interesting work in pleasant working conditions.

Please apply in writing only with predicted exam results or qualifications to the address above

REED EDUCATIONAL & PROFESSIONAL PUBLISHING

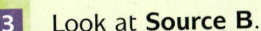

Hours	Rate	£.pp	Deductions	£.pp	Year to
		1458.34	Tax	235.34	Gross Pay
			National Ins.	104.71	Taxable Pe
			Pension	38.20	Tax Paid
					National Ins
					Pension

9456.00
1536.12
590.97
252.40

* BALANCES *

Working to live?

All human labour is work. You are, or should be, working at the moment! So not all work is paid. When people are paid for their work it is called employment. In More Economically Developed Countries (MEDCs) most people of working age are formally employed or looking for employment. They may be employed by others or **self-employed**.

C *Employment opportunities have changed?*

The Ironbridge Chronicle – 1895

BLACKSMITH wanted; to live in; used to country work and a good shoer. – Apply, GEORGE FOXALL, Stableford, Bridgnorth.

COWMAN wanted; steady middle-aged man preferred; must be good milker; cottage with large garden found close to work; state wages. Also respectable Youth. – GEO. KEY, Kings Heath Farm, Birmingham.

GENERAL Servant (good) Wanted, not under 20; good home for respectable woman. – PALMER, Fishmonger, Wellington.

Formal employment: a person who is formally employed receives a wage or salary from their employer. They usually have a contract that gives them certain rights, like a wage during holidays and periods when they are sick. They also have responsibilities like the need to attend work every day. A person who is formally employed pays taxes and has other deductions made from their pay at **source**.

B

D

Informal employment: a person who is informally employed does not receive a regular wage. They work when they need to or when they feel like it. There are sometimes no deductions made from their earnings but if they do not work, for whatever reason, they receive no payment.

3 Look at **Source B**.
  a Make a list of ways in which money is taken from employed people 'at source'.
  b Suggest how the person may benefit from each deduction.

4 Look at **Source C**.
  a Compare the jobs in *The Ironbridge Chronicle* with those shown in **Source B**.
  b Suggest why employment opportunities change with time.

5 Look at **Source D** and page 5.
  a Describe the work in both photographs.
  b What do you feel about these scenes? Explain your feelings.
  c List other jobs that involve informal employment.

6 a What are the advantages and disadvantages of formal and informal employment?
  b Which would you prefer? Why?

This 12-year-old boy is sorting glass in Guatemala

1.2 A north–south divide?

How do employment opportunities change over time?

What regional variations in quality of life and standards of living exist in the UK?

What evidence is there for a north-south divide in the UK?

A Working in a Lancashire cotton mill.

The north of England relied on work in heavy industries such as coal, steel, shipbuilding and textile production. Many of these jobs have been lost in the last 40 years causing high unemployment and changes in building use.

B New opportunities?

Former cotton mills have changed their function, retail outlets Many are now warehouses, retail outlets or have been turned into flats. These provide fewer job opportunities than their traditional use.

C Percentage unemployed by UK standard regions

1961

Key
- Over 12%
- 10.1 – 12%
- 8.1 – 10%
- 8% or less

1996

In 1999, the North East (10.1%) and London (7.6%) had the highest unemployment rates. All other regions were below 7%, with the South East being the lowest at 3.6%.

D UK wealth by region 1998 Gross Domestic Product per head

100 = Average UK index for GDP per head

Source: Regional Trends 2000

Gross Domestic Product (GDP) per person is the total value of goods and services produced by a country or region in one year divided by the total number of people living in that country or region. It may be used as an indicator of economic development.

The *Rich North* and *Poor South* are terms that have been applied to the world when talking about economic development. In the United Kingdom (UK), the reverse has often been the case. Some people will argue that life in the UK is dominated by London and that the further north you go, the poorer life becomes. What evidence is there for and against this view?

1
a Describe the scenes in **Sources A** and **B**.
b How has the function of traditional factory buildings changed during the past half-century?
c Suggest how these changes have affected job opportunities and the lives of people in the north of England.

2
a Describe the 1961 pattern of employment in **Source C**.
b What changes had taken place:
  • by 1996 • by 1999?
c Comment on your findings.

3 Look at **Source D**. Use evidence from the graph and **Source C** to answer the question 'Was there a divide between the north and the south in the UK in the late 1990s?'

	England and Wales	North East	London region
Infant mortality rate per 1000 live births	5.8	5.4	5.9
% pupils achieving 5+ GCSE grades A* to C	49.2	40.8	46.7
Average house price	£94 581	£59 442	£150 094
Average weekly earnings	£399	£349	£520
Recorded crime rates per 100 000 population	9785	10 359	12 354
Local taxes as % of income	2.9	3.4	2.3

Source: Regional Trends 2000

 E Standard of living indicators

G The Northumberland National Park is easily accessible from

H The journey to work in the London region can be stressful and time-consuming. The average journey takes 32 minutes. In the north east it is 20 minutes.

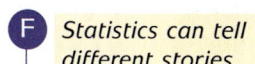 F Statistics can tell different stories...

NORTH-SOUTH DIVIDE IS GETTING SMALLER

Government research shows the north-south divide is getting smaller. This is because those earning most in London and the south east have to spend more on soaring housing and transport costs. House prices have increased by 17% in London compared with 6% in the north east. Average household expenditure in London is £376.40 compare with only £282.90 in the north east. Consequently receiving a lower income in the north east does not always mean you are worse off after living costs have been considered.

Adapted from The Times, 28 September 2000

North-South divide at all time high

Britain's north-south divide is at its widest on record. Figures from the Office of National Statistics show that London and the south east have become significantly more wealthy relative to the north than in 1989, the peak of the divide under the Conservative government. GDP indicators show that Londoners are 59% better off than those in the north east – the poorest region – compared with 43% in 1989. There is a lower percentage of jobs in the north-east and more people claim income support.

Adapted from The Times, 28 March 2001

DURHAM

A first class County

QUALITY OF LIFE

A good location for business must also be a good location in which to live.

County Durham offers many of the ingredients for an enjoyable lifestyle-unspoilt countryside, a range of cultural activities, attractive housing and a choice of good education.

The area has many attractions for lovers of the outdoors – walking, riding, fishing, golf – but there is plenty to entertain those who prefer to relex and watch others. World Class Athletics, Cricket, Premier League Football and the international RAC motor rally are just some of the sporting events to be held in the area

4 Look at **Source E**.
a Rank the standard of living indicators according to how important you think they are. Explain your chosen order.
b Draw graphs to compare the North East and London regions for your **three** most important indicators.

5 Read the articles in **Source F** and your answer to task 3b.
a What evidence suggests the north-south divide is:
  • getting smaller
  • getting larger?
b Suggest why there is a difference in the opinions about what is happening to the divide.
c Select **four** statistics you would use in deciding whether there is a north-south divide. Justify your choice.
d What other factors might you consider important when comparing regions as a place to live? Explain your choices.

6 Use **Sources G** and **H** and other information on these pages to decide whether the North East or London might offer you the better:
  • standard of living
  • quality of life.
Explain your choice.

Two extremes?

There are many **standard of living** indicators. They are all features of a region or country that can be measured. **Quality of life** is about those aspects of life that are difficult to measure, such as a person's health, happiness, friendships and service to others. These are more important to many people than having possessions. Having a high quality of life does not necessarily depend on a high standard of living but it may be difficult to achieve if the standard of living is very low.

1.3 International patterns

Employment structures

Employment may be classified according to the kind of work that is done. There are three main employment types or sectors.

Primary: the sector of a country's economy that grows or extracts raw materials. It includes fishing, forestry, agriculture and the extraction of minerals.

Secondary: the sector of a country's economy that is concerned with the manufacturing and processing of goods. It uses the products of primary industry either directly or indirectly. For example, coal, iron ore and limestone are used *directly* to make steel. They are then used *indirectly* when steel is used in the many engineering industries, like the assembly of cars.

Tertiary: the sector of a country's economy that provides a service. People may pay directly for the service, as in the case of a taxi ride. Other services, such as National Health Service hospitals, are paid for indirectly by taking **National Insurance** contributions from a person's income.

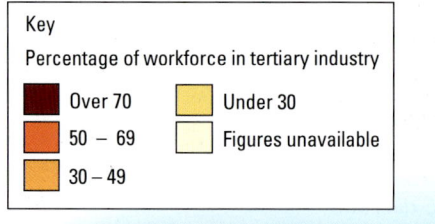

A Winnowing wheat, India

B Car manufacturing production line, Europe

C Tram driver, Hong Kong

1 a Describe what is happening in each of **Sources A, B** and **C**.
  b Match each to its correct employment sector.
  c Add other examples of jobs in each employment sector.

2 Look at **Source D**.
  a Describe the distribution of those countries having the greater percentage of their workforce in the tertiary sector.
  b Compare this with the distribution of those having the fewest.
  c Suggest why the percentage employed in the tertiary sector is used as an indicator of economic development.

Key
Percentage of workforce in tertiary industry

■ Over 70	□ Under 30
■ 50 – 69	□ Figures unavailable
■ 30 – 49	

D *Percentage of total workforce employed in the tertiary sector in 2000. The percentage employed in these service industries is taken as an indicator of economic development.*

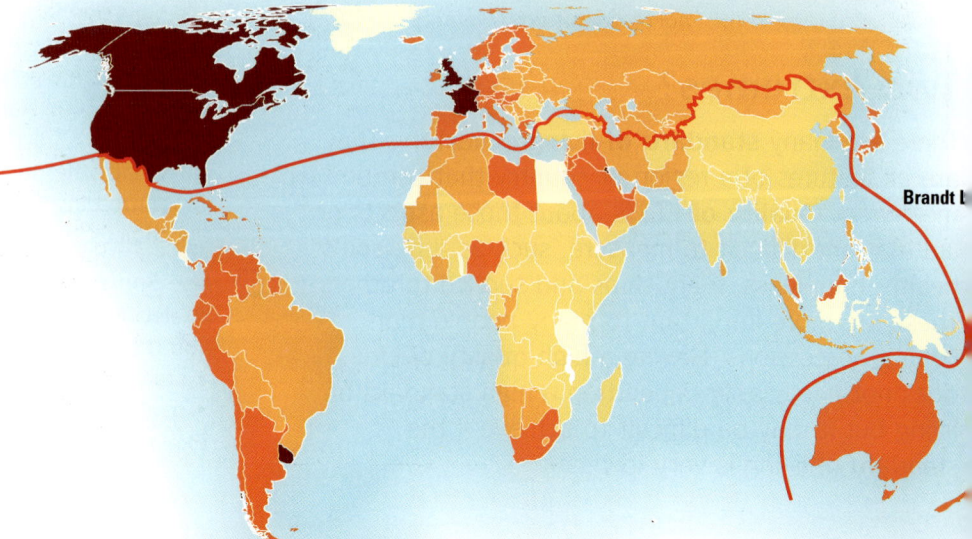

Brandt L

Changes with time

Employment structures change over time E

	Primary		Secondary		Tertiary	
	1975	**1999**	**1975**	**1999**	**1975**	**1999**
UK	3	2	31	29	66	69
France	10	6	28	29	62	65
Mexico	41	28	20	24	39	48

(Figures show the percentage of the workforce in each sector.)　　Source: UNESCO

	Primary		Secondary		Tertiary	
	M	**F**	**M**	**F**	**M**	**F**
UK	3	1	38	13	59	86
France	6	4	37	15	57	81
Mexico	30	13	24	19	46	68

(Figures show the percentage of workforce in each sector.)

*Employment by **gender** 1999* F

As a country develops its economy, the proportion of its workforce in the different employment sectors changes. Using more machinery in farming, for example, releases people from working the land and frees them to be employed in other ways. Likewise, the use of machinery in manufacturing enables a greater proportion of the workers to be involved in providing services. A country that is in the early stages of economic development is called a Less Economically Developed Country (LEDC) and a country that is in the later stages of such development is called a More Economically Developed Country (MEDC).

G *Changing employment patterns in India*

1975

Tertiary 18%
Secondary 10%
Primary 72%

1999

Tertiary 20%
Secondary 16%
Primary 64%

Key
■ Male
■ Female

Percentage employed

Primary　Secondary　Tertiary

Employment by gender 1999

Computer analysts, Bangalore, India H

Source: Financial Times

Message from the
Prime Minister

IT is India's Tomorrow

Information Technology is one of the greatest boons to science and humanity. It is revolutionising life on this planet like no other technology has in human history. It has been impacting on the economy, communication, culture, educational system and social interaction in all the countries, bringing them closer in a world transformed into a Global Village and laying the foundation for a new civilisation. India, as the cradle of civilisation, is poised to become a major IT power in the coming years and contribute to the realisation of its many promises for our benefit and for the global good.

3 Look at **Source E**.
  a Place the countries in rank order using employment structure as an indicator of economic development in 1999.
  b Which country appears to have developed the most rapidly between 1975 and 1999?
  c What evidence justifies your choice?

4 a Use information from **Sources E** and **F** to draw graphs for the UK similar to those for India in **Source G**.
  b Compare the graphs.
  c Suggest reasons for any similarities and differences you have described.

5 a Use **Sources G** and **H** to describe the employment changes that are taking place in India.
  b To what extent do you think India is making progress towards becoming an MEDC?

1.4 Technology is changing work patterns

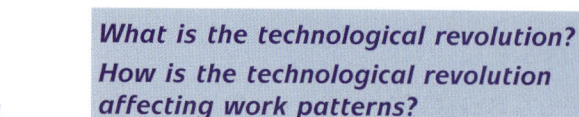

A rapidly changing world

Developments in Information and Communications Technology (ICT) towards the end of the twentieth century have begun to have a marked impact on the way people work. Not only have employment opportunities been created in manufacturing hardware and software, but the way in which the Internet allows us to communicate instantly with almost anywhere in the world has also affected work patterns.

 A *ICT – India's path to economic progress?*

Silicon Valley in California and the Silicon Glen in Scotland are areas that have gained employment opportunities from the technological revolution. Nowhere, though, has the impact been so great as in India. India is the leading software development centre for many of the world's leading ICT firms. It offers them:

- highly skilled workers
- a developing communications structure
- relatively low labour costs
- high-quality finished products
- global continuity of work for 24 hours: when it is evening in the USA it is morning in India.

B *The development of technology manufacturing in India*

INDIA ON THE GLOBAL ECONOMIC MAP

India is finally getting her fair share of attention and is firmly on the radar screen of the new technology. In case you missed it, a major news item last week was AOL's announcement that it plans to spend $100 million to establish a development centre in Bangalore. AOL joins a list of familiar names: IBM, Cisco and MIT's Media Lab

Adapted from an article by Raj Merchant,
Siliconindia.com, 27 February 2001

Bill Gates in India on his second visit

Microsoft Corporation Chairman and Chief Software Architect, Bill Gates, landed in New Delhi on Wednesday evening in his private jetliner for his second visit to India, signalling the importance the world's largest software house attaches to the country…

(Indiaexpress.com, 13 September 2000)

 C *India's top ten companies 1995–1999*

1995	1999
1 Lever	Lever
2 Reliance Industries	Wipro *(ICT)*
3 Tata Engineering	Infosys Technologies *(ICT)*
4 Tata Iron and Steel	Reliance Industries
5 Indian Tobacco Co.	Zee Telefilms
6 Larsen and Toubro	Indian Tobacco Co.
7 Bajaj Auto	Ranbaxy Laboratories
8 Grasim Industries	Larsen and Toubro
9 Hindalco	Nilt *(ICT)*
10 Whirlpool	Satyam Computer Services *(ICT)*

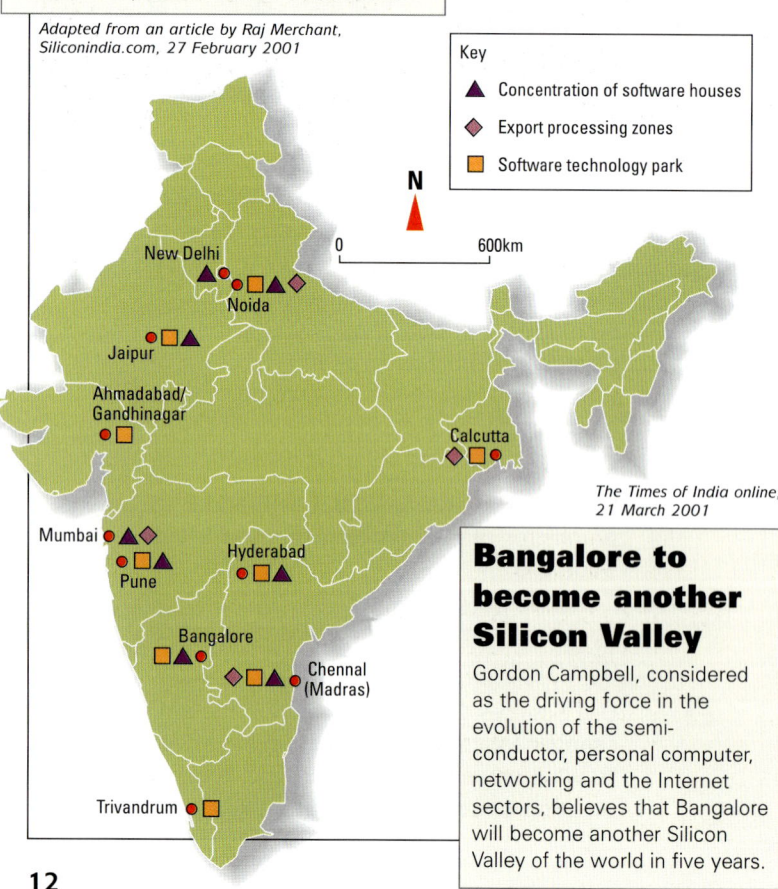

Key
- ▲ Concentration of software houses
- ◆ Export processing zones
- ■ Software technology park

New Delhi
Noida
Jaipur
Ahmadabad/Gandhinagar
Calcutta
Mumbai
Pune
Hyderabad
Bangalore
Chennai (Madras)
Trivandrum

The Times of India online, 21 March 2001

Bangalore to become another Silicon Valley

Gordon Campbell, considered as the driving force in the evolution of the semiconductor, personal computer, networking and the Internet sectors, believes that Bangalore will become another Silicon Valley of the world in five years.

1
a What do you understand by the term ICT?
b Give **three** ways in which recent ICT developments have affected your life.

2 Study **Source A**.
a List the attractions of India for ICT firms.
b Explain why each attraction is an advantage.

3
a Use the map in **Source B** to describe the distribution of software houses.
b Suggest why they are concentrated in only a few centres.
c Explain how the news articles support the view that ICT is *India's path to economic progress*.

4
a Describe the changes shown in **Source C**.
b How do these changes support your answer to 3c?

Technology serves the people

 D *DoctorAnywhere.com*

Connecting doctors and specialists in India

DoctorsAnywhere.com is India's first and only Internet-based doctor-to-doctor consultation service. Since its start in 1999, thirteen States and Union Territories have been incorporated in the network covering over 200 towns and cities. With a population as big as India's, the resource of 40 medical specialists, concentrated in the 35 major towns and cities, is a support needed by doctors all over the country. Patients face a lot of stress and spend time and money in order to get a specialist's opinion. Using DoctorsAnywhere.com patients can get the opinions of leading specialists without having to travel.

Source: DoctorsAnywhere.com

 E *Increasing farming choices*

The area: Coastal Gujarat near Mumbai, an area of limestone where over-irrigation has caused salt water in the soil. Current farming is unsustainable.

Main crops: Sugar cane and groundnuts. Both require heavy irrigation.

Role of ICT: Using the telephone and the Internet, everyday farm prices in Mumbai for different crops that could be grown in the area and that required less irrigation were displayed to the farmers. The profits for these crops were worked out.

The result: All farmers could see how to make greater profit by changing their farming habits. Some adopted more sustainable cropping patterns.

 G *Frustration for the commuter*

People are increasingly working from home. The journey to work has become a nightmare for many and they are looking at the option of working via the Internet.
Some have decided to migrate from their former homes and work from a telecottage. There are over 70 in the remoter parts of the UK, such as the Highlands and Islands of Scotland. Employers feel that they can save between £6 000 and £20 000 a year for each employee who chooses telecottaging.

Casual Friday for the Telecommuter

F *Virtually there!*

One day a government official came in a jeep. He was treated like a king … He said that the government was going to set up a kiosk with computers. Farmers would be able to access land records and rates of agricultural produce from markets across the country in no time. The latest government schemes for development would become more accessible. Educating children would become easier.

Could it be true? Information, the villagers knew, was always locked away in the files of the *patwari* (keeper of land records) and he always demanded money. The old-timers refused to give credence to all this compu-talk … The electricity supply was as infrequent as the rains. And there wasn't a 'phone line in a radius of 10km.

Adapted from Down to Earth, Vol. 9, No. 18, 15 February 2001

5 Use **Sources D** and **E** to help explain how technology is:
- affecting the way people work in India
- helping people in India.

6 a What other ways does **Source F** suggest people in India's rural areas may benefit from ICT? Add some ideas of your own.
   b What needs to happen before many Indian villagers can take full advantage of the Technological Revolution?

7 Study **Source G**.
   a Explain the benefits and drawbacks of working from home. Refer to standard of living and quality of life.
   b 'The Technological Revolution will change all our working patterns.' To what extent do you agree with this statement?

1 Count me in-Census 2001

count me in
Census2001

Census is a Latin word meaning 'count'

A census enumerator is appointed to deliver forms to about 150 households in a ward. Very little interrupts the census. It did not, though, happen in 1941 due to the Second World War.

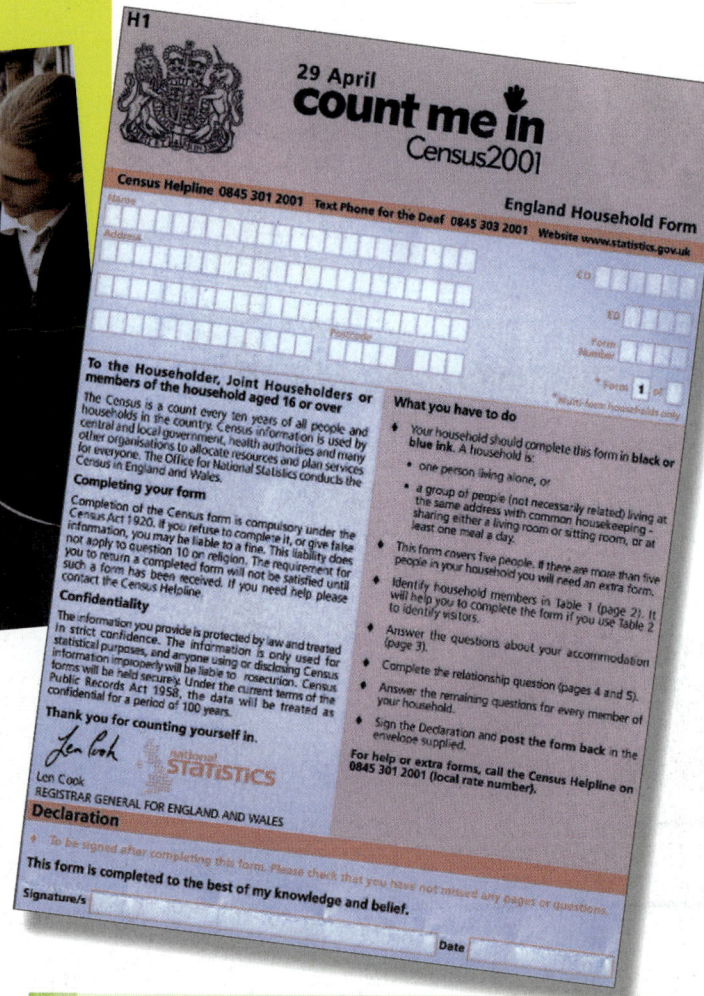

The UK Census – Sunday 29 April 2001

To find out about work and employment, as well as other data, a census is carried out in the UK every ten years. The first census was in 1801 when the government wanted to know how much food to produce. The most recent census was on 29 April 2001. The census form contained 41 questions which had to be completed by householders for that day.

Census information is only correct on the day it is recorded but processing the data takes at least a year. By the time it is published it is out-of-date! With the use of ICT, however, the 2001 results will be published more quickly than for previous censuses.

Organising a census costs money. The UK's 2001 census cost £255 million. Wealthy countries can afford to have regular censuses that can be completed for one specific date. However many poorer countries cannot afford this. They use a great deal of guesswork to provide data. Sometimes, due to poor communication links, it is collected over several weeks or months. Some countries are so poor they do not carry out a census, or events in the country make it impossible to do.

1
a What does the word 'census' mean?
b How frequently are UK censuses carried out?
c When will the next UK census take place?

2
a What does a census enumerator do?
b Suggest why the census date is a Sunday in the UK.

3
a Suggest why some census data might be unreliable.
b Completing and returning the census form in the UK is a legal requirement. What is your view on this?

4
a Organise and analyse a mini-census for your class.
b Visit the website www.heinemann.co.uk/hotlinks. Investigate work and employment trends for your local area and region.

5
Imagine you are in charge of organizing a census in an LEDC. Suggest **five** issues that you would want to collect data on. Justify your choices.

2

Development, trade and aid

KEY IDEAS

Economic and social well-being can be measured using a variety of indicators.

Development means more than economic development.

International trade and aid have contributed to contrasting stages of development.

Students at a new IT school in a favela in Rio de Janeiro, Brazil

2.1 What is development?

The haves and have-nots?

As a result of **the Brandt Report** in 1980, an imaginary line was drawn on world maps. This line divides countries into:

- More Economically Developed Countries (MEDCs)
- Less Economically Developed Countries (LEDCs).

Different terms and definitions have been used to describe 'development'. These may change again as the present MEDC/LEDC division is challenged. In the early years of the twenty-first century, many of Brandt's LEDCs will be approaching or have reached MEDC status.

Whatever definitions of development are used, some countries have greater economic wealth and a higher quality of life than others. But even if economic development is weak, countries can show great social and cultural development.

Heads...

Economic development...

Cultural development...

A

Social development...

...and tails

...refers to works of art, music, customs, rites and religious or spiritual aspects that develop in a society.

...refers to the wealth of a community. This can be measured by economic indicators such as average income and home ownership.

...refers to the way people work with and for each other in a community. This includes strong family ties, and a caring attitude towards each other and the environment.

The world according to the Brandt report (1980)

'Development is more than the passage from poor to rich, from a traditional rural economy to a sophisticated urban one. It carries with it not only the idea of economic betterment, but also of greater human dignity, security, justice and equity.'

Willy Brandt (1980)

Willy Brandt, Chancellor of West Germany 1968–74, chaired the Commission on International Development which decided the location of the North–South line.

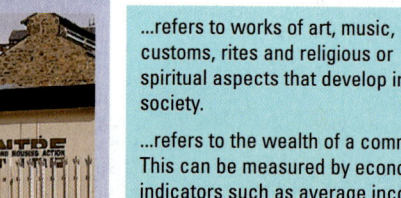

B

The Brandt Line

Peru

Kenya

China

Key
- MEDCs
- LEDCs

Peru: Music from Peru using pan-pipes has developed over many centuries. It is possible to buy CDs of this pan-pipe music.

CHINA: The Great Wall of China is 2 400 km long. It was begun in the third century by Emperor Shih Huang Ti to keep out enemies. To plan and complete it required an organized society of great skill and human resources.

KENYA: Tribal customs and initiation ceremonies often involve face decoration. Such traditions are part of African culture. They have been passed down through many generations.

---

1 Describe each scene in **Source A** and match each head to its tail.

2 Study the captions around **Source B**.
  a Are these countries regarded as MEDCs or LEDCs by Brandt?
  b What evidence suggests these countries are or were socially or culturally developed?

3 Read Willy Brandt's comment in **Source B**.
  a What do you understand by the terms:
  - human dignity
  - justice
  - security
  - equity?
  b Explain what is meant by 'Development is more than the passage from poor to rich'. Do you agree with this view? Why?

C

- Gross National Product (GNP) per head
- Life expectancy
- Value of exports
- Children per woman
- Access to health services
- TV sets per 1000 people
- Oil consumption per person
- Value of imports

Indicators of economic and social well-being

Indicators of economic and social well-being (2000)

	UK	PERU
GNP per head ($)	21 410	2 350
Exports (million $)	367 971	7 506
Imports (million $)	374 045	10 483
Oil consumption per person (kg)	3 683	621
Life expectancy (years)	77	69
Children per woman	1.7	2.9
Access to health services (%)	100	44
TV sets (per 1000 people)	806	142

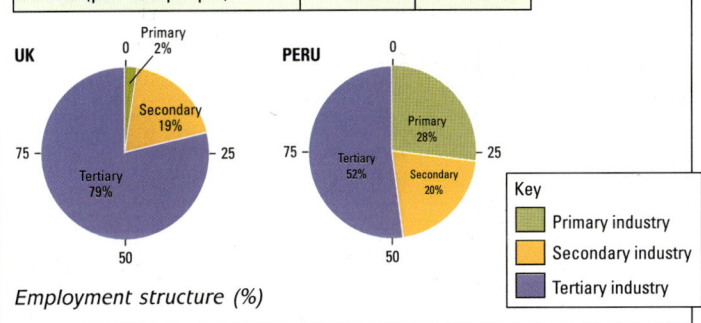

UK
Primary 2%
Secondary 19%
Tertiary 79%

PERU
Primary 28%
Secondary 20%
Tertiary 52%

Key
- Primary industry
- Secondary industry
- Tertiary industry

Employment structure (%)

D *Comparing development indicators in the UK (an MEDC) with Peru (an LEDC)*

4 Study **Source C**.
  a How are economic and social well-being different?
  b Make a two-column table: one column for economic well-being, one for social well-being. Place the eight indicators in **Source C** into the column you think they fit best.
  c Add **two** other measures to each column that you think would be useful in deciding a country's economic and social well-being.

5 Use evidence from **Sources D** and **E** to justify the UK being classified as an MEDC and Peru as an LEDC.

6 a Choose **six** measurable indicators that you would use to decide if a country was 'developed'? Include economic, social and cultural indicators.
  b Suggest other criteria that are not easily measured.
  c To what extent is Peru a developed country according to your indicators?

7 You have to choose **six** images and/or objects for an exhibition called 'The United Kingdom: an economically, socially and culturally developed country'.
  a Choose your images and/or objects.
  b List images and/or objects you would **not** choose. Explain why.

Parris visits Peru

Columnist and broadcaster Matthew Parris has visited Peru several times in recent years. **Source E** shows some observations from his book *Inca Kola*.

E *Some aspects of development in Peru*

Economic development

Peruvians were desperate for dollars. Their own currency was inflating so fast that savings lost their value almost as you watched. The government had fixed the international value of their currency artificially high so that foreigners would have to bring more dollars into Peru and get fewer Peruvian *intis* in exchange.

Few Peruvians own cars. People of all walks of life must use buses: and for most they are the only means of reaching distant places.

Social development

We sat down, some on the floor, some on chairs. Candles were lit and the rest of Nazario's family came in. Nazario introduced them proudly. His father was called Elias, his mother Apolonia. His three sisters were Doris, Gladys and Iris. His little brother was Adolfo, and their aunt, Wilma, from Chiquian, was also staying ... You soon got used to the fact that, without electricity, let alone television, nightfall is soon followed by bed.

Cultural development

One exhibit, though, stayed in the mind. Among a scattering of mummies stood a feathered skull ... to which had been glued thousands of tiny, soft, blue and yellow parrot feathers. Though centuries old, the feathers, brilliance had kept alive their colours ... It was supposed to be spine-tingling. It was supposed to be grotesque, chilling and beautiful ... like their haunting flute music. And, like the music, it was.

2.2 Rule Britannia?

The good old days?

Today the United Kingdom (UK) is regarded as a More Economically Developed Country (MEDC). Much of Britain's early economic wealth and economic development came from colonies established all over the world in the sixteenth and seventeenth centuries. This helped it become the **First Industrial Nation** in the eighteenth and nineteenth centuries.

Until 1833, Britain seized people and took them against their will from West Africa to the islands of the West Indies and the southern USA. Here they worked as slaves on plantations. Britain then imported raw materials such as rum, sugar, and cotton from these colonies. Manufactured goods were exported to the colonies in exchange. This 'slave triangle' formed the basis of early international trade, mostly to the advantage of Britain.

Key
The British Empire in 1914

Map labels: CANADA, UNITED KINGDOM, Bermuda, Bahamas, British Honduras, Jamaica, Leeward Is, Barbados, Trinidad, British Guiana, Falkland Is, South Georgia, Gibraltar, Gambia, Sierra Leone, Gold Coast, Malta, Cyprus, Egypt, Nigeria, Anglo Egyptian Sudan, Buganda, British East Africa, South Rhodesia, Bechuanaland, Cape Province, Orange Free State, Natal, Transvaai, North Rhodesia, Nyasaland, British Somaliland, Baluchistan, INDIA, Upper Burma, Burma, Malaya, Borneo, Papua New Guinea, Fiji, AUSTRALIA, NEW ZEALAND

The British Empire Ⓐ

Ⓒ **Britain and its colonies**

An overseer supervises slaves working in the fields Ⓑ

What Britain wanted from its colonies

Object 1: To exploit the natural resources.
Object 2: To expand markets for manufactured goods.
Object 3: To use land and labour to grow crops.

How Britain changed the colonies

• Farming and food supply
Local people changed from growing food crops to cash crops for colonial powers, e.g. sugar, cotton, rubber, tobacco. The best land became cash crop plantations. There was less land for food crops so self-sufficiency was reduced. The colony became vulnerable to food shortages. With no food resources to survive people became dependent on the colonial power.

• Manufacturing
Colonial powers sold their own manufactured goods in colonies. This destroyed traditional industry in colonies. Only one or two export goods were left; usually a mineral or cash crop.
The colony was vulnerable to price changes and falling demand.

• Government
After colonization new country boundaries were based on European agreements not on ethnic, regional or historical ones. Many tribal groups in West Africa were separated and mixed within one colony leading to local rivalry.

Trading people

Portuguese traders first developed the idea of sending labourers from Africa to the Americas. The first slave ship sailed in 1510. Captain John Hawkins took the first British slave ship to the British West Indies in 1562. Some Britons grew wealthy from selling slaves and from the use of slave labour. Britain abolished slavery in 1833.

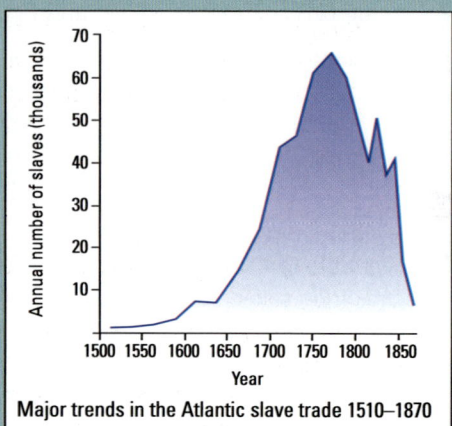

Major trends in the Atlantic slave trade 1510–1870

(Graph: Annual number of slaves (thousands) vs Year, 1500–1850)

1. Study **Source A**.
   a. Describe the distribution of British colonies in 1914.
   b. There was a time when it was said that 'The sun never sets on the British Empire'. What do you think this means?

2. Study **Source B**.
   a. Describe the trends in the Atlantic slave trade:
      • before 1750
      • between 1750 and 1855.
   b. When did Britain abolish slavery?
   c. List reasons why slavery is wrong.

3. Study **Source C**.
   a. List what Britain wanted from its colonies.
   b. Produce a storyboard to show how farming and manufacturing changed in the colonies.
   c. How were the boundaries of West African colonies decided?
   d. Suggest how these agreements:
      • benefited the development of European economies
      • held back the development of West African countries.

Independence: blessing or curse?

After the Second World War (1939-1945), Britain and the rest of Western Europe began to co-operate more closely. To encourage economic recovery, money was spent at home rather than abroad.

Many British colonies took this opportunity to regain their **independence**. For countries such as Botswana, independence has been a positive experience. Its economy has grown and progress has been made in health and welfare. For countries such as Ghana and Sierra Leone, however, independence has been a mixed blessing.

D *Ghana and Sierra Leone lead the way ... to independence*

'Without exception the imperialists left us nothing but our resentment'

Kwame Nkrumah

In 1957, Ghana became the first African country to win its independence from Britain. Kwame Nkrumah was the first President of Ghana from 1957-1968. In 1961, Sierra Leone followed Ghana in gaining its independence.

Independence day celebrations in Sierra Leone

Sierra Leone was left with an established infrastructure built by the British. There were roads, railways, ports, and bridges. Our companies had discovered mineral wealth and established mines as well as plantations. We continued to provide a market for minerals and cash crops after independence. We also introduced a framework for education and justice based on British ideas.

British claims **E**

F *The state of the countries in 1999*

Comparative indicators between past years and 1999

	Life expectancy (years)		Adult literacy (%)		Access to safe water (%)	
	1960	1999	1970	1999	1980	1999
Ghana	45	60	31	64	35	65
Sierra Leone	31	38	13	31	14	38
UK		77		99		99

Economic and social indicators 1999

Indicator	UK	Ghana	Sierra Leone
GNP per head ($)	21 410	390	140
Urban/rural (%)	90/10	37/63	35/65
Children per woman	1.7	5.1	6
Daily calorie supply per person	3 237	2 560	2 002
TV sets per 1000 people	806	41	17

Employment structure (% employed) 1999

	UK	Ghana	Sierra Leone
Primary industry	2	60	68
Secondary industry	19	13	15
Tertiary industry	79	27	17

4 Study **Source D**.
a What was significant about Ghana's independence?
b What was the attitude of President Nkrumah towards Britain?
c When did Sierra Leone gain its independence?
d Suggest why the people of Ghana and Sierra Leone wanted independence from Britain.

5 Study **Sources E and G**.
a What does Britain claim to have left Sierra Leone with?
b Suggest which of these features:
  • should have helped Sierra Leone develop its economy after independence.
  • may have worked against its development after independence.

6 Study **Sources F and G**.
a Draw graphs to compare:
  • changes in the indicators between past years and 1999 in Ghana and Sierra Leone
  • UK indicators with those of Ghana and Sierra Leone for 1999.
b Discuss whether independence has been a 'blessing or a curse' for *either* Ghana *or* Sierra Leone. Use evidence to support your argument.

G *Two countries compared: progress since independence*

GHANA 1957-2000
• Early independence favoured the owners of large cocoa plantations. Much of the profit went out of the country or to a corrupt government. However, since 1980, after tribal conflicts, Ghana has known peace and stability.
• In recent years a huge migration to the cities has resulted in the growth of shanty towns. Over half of all Ghanaians will live in cities by 2020.
• Rainforest once covered 34 per cent of the country; now only a quarter of this is left.
• Economic development has been affected by an energy crisis, low gold prices, poor harvests and competition due to cheap imports from Taiwan, China and South Korea.
• Low rainfall and a drop in the level of water behind the Akosombo dam means that Ghana is paying to import electricity from Cote d'Ivoire.
• Ghana intends to be a middle-income country through its Vision 2020 programme.
• **Ghana has an HDI* rank of 133/174.**

SIERRA LEONE 1961-2000
• Sierra Leone, like many other African countries, was created by Europeans. This forced together rival tribal groups within the country's borders. Tribal rivalry has prevented stable government.
• Corruption is widespread.
• Exports have fallen and debt increased.
• Food such as rice is scarce
• Over one million people have lost their homes due to civil war.
• Extreme poverty has caused young children to be traded as servants to families in the Middle East. They do not all return.
• Multi-national companies used to control much of the gold and diamond mining. In 1998 these companies were evicted.
• Since 1995 the civil war has involved UN troops and hostage-taking by rebels. There is no stable government.
• **Sierra Leone has an HDI* rank of 174 – the lowest rank of all.**

*HDI = Human Development Index: a measure of achievement in a country based on life expectancy, education and standard of living.

2.3 Several countries – one Europe

Trading closer to home

No country can be totally **self-sufficient** in all its needs. Countries need to trade with each other. The UK still trades with its former colonies but, over the last 40 years, these links have become weaker.

This is partly because the UK joined the **European Economic Community (EEC)** in 1973. After the Second World War (1939-1945) many countries in Western Europe wanted peace and stability. They began to work and trade together and share decision-making. This organisation, now known as the **European Union (EU)**, had fifteen member states in 2001 with others applying to join.

We've had enough! **A**

To join or not to join ...

*Edward Heath was Prime Minister of the Conservative government from 1969 to 1974. He feared that if the UK, as an island, did not join the EEC it would be isolated from other European countries. They would work together and develop their economies and the UK would suffer. In 1975 the newly elected Labour Government held a **referendum** to see whether people wanted to stay in the EEC. The majority did!*

Prime Minister Edward Heath signs the agreement to commit the UK to join the EEC from 1 January 1973 **C**

D The Community grows

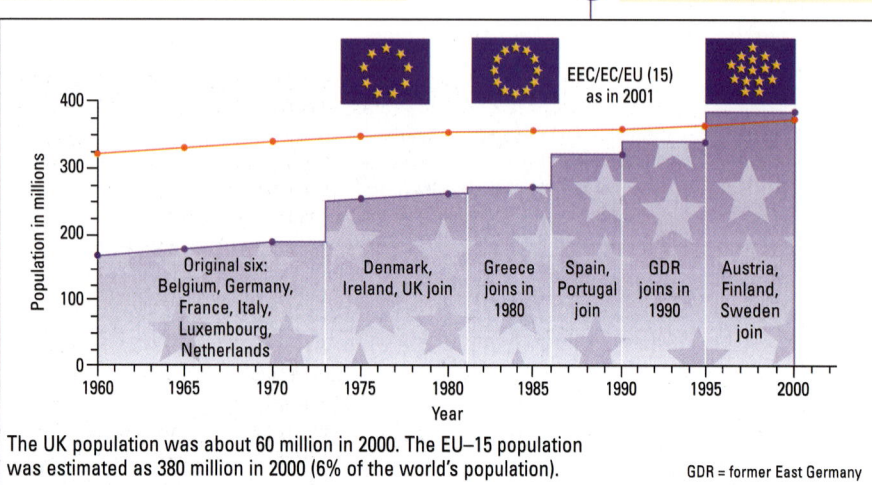

The UK population was about 60 million in 2000. The EU–15 population was estimated as 380 million in 2000 (6% of the world's population).

GDR = former East Germany

1948: Belgium, Netherlands and Luxembourg, recovering from war, formed an economic union known as Benelux.

1952: France, Germany and Italy joined with Benelux to form the **European Coal and Steel Community (ECSC)**. Agreements were made about coal and steel production and trade.

1 January 1958: the EEC was founded as a trading group. It was also known as 'The Common Market'. Members could:

- trade cheaply or freely with each other;
- share greater security together to avoid future conflict;
- have a stronger voice in international trade with other large powerful groups.

B From small beginnings

---

1 Use **Sources A** and **B** to suggest why some countries in Western Europe wished to work together after 1945.

2 Study **Source C**.
  a Give reasons why Edward Heath wanted the UK to join the EEC.
  b What is a 'referendum'? Suggest why the Labour government held one in 1975.
  c Suggest one other issue for which the UK government might wish to use a referendum. Justify your choice.

3 Study **Source D**.
  a On an outline map of Europe shade in different colours the groups of countries that:
    • formed the EEC
    • joined between 1973 and 1981
    • joined between 1981 and 1990
    • joined after 1995.
  b What was unusual about the country that 'joined' in 1990?
  c 'There is safety in numbers.' Use evidence from the graph to discuss this statement.

Europe all around us **E**

Human rights

Soccer players free to move within EU

Following an appeal by Marc Bosnan, the Anderlecht player, the world of European soccer is set for major transfer moves. The court has ruled that once players have reached the end of their contract, they can move on free transfers to other clubs within the EU.

Land-use

Oil seed rape and linseed change UK farmscape

The farming landscape of the UK is becoming dominated by the yellow of oil-seed rape and the blue of linseed oil. The EU is giving grants to farmers for crops it needs in EU countries. It is also paying farmers not to grow wheat and to set aside land for conservation to allow meadows and new woodland to grow.

Welcome to **BROUGHTON ASTLEY** Twinned with Gévezé

Britain to join new EU army

Britain is to send troops to join the EU army from 2002. The rapid reaction force will be used for peacekeeping and emergency missions where NATO does not want to be involved.

Military co-operation

Transport

The Channel Tunnel linking the UK to the rest of Europe was opened in 1994

Convicted criminal appeals to European Court of Justice in Strasbourg

Law

The euro became the EU's common currency on 1 January 1999. Three EU countries (Britain, Denmark and Sweden) are delaying its introduction and keeping their own currency. The other twelve EU countries are replacing their currency with euros from 1 January 2002 affecting 290 million people. Already UK companies accept payment in euros and any British individual can open a euro bank account. The British government has promised a referendum on replacing pounds and pence with euros after the 2001 General Election

...and in future?

French not ready for euro?

The 1st January 2002 sees the launch of euro coins and notes and seven weeks later, from 17th February 2002, there will be no more francs in France. But are the French ready? Surveys show that 40 per cent of the French do not feel ready. Recently, 50 000 electricity and gas customers were sent their bills in euros and wrote cheques for the same amount in francs. The companies were alarmed as francs are worth less than one sixth of the euro…

---

4 Study **Source E**.
a List the examples of EU influence shown.
b Find others and add them to your list.

5 Study **Sources F** and **G**.
a How many EU countries will be using the euro from 2002?
b Which countries are delaying replacing their currency with the euro?
c What difficulties are likely to be experienced when a currency is changed?
d Do you think Britain should replace pounds and pence with the euro? Justify your view using **Source G** and your own ideas.

6 'We are all Europeans now.' To what extent do you agree with this statement?

F *In comes the euro… slowly*

G *The euro – some arguments for and against the UK using it*

Advantages for Britain	Disadvantages for Britain
• For travellers there will be no need to change currency when crossing EU borders.	• If a high interest rate suits the other EU countries but not Britain, this may lead to businesses closing and high unemployment here.
• With the same currency it will be easy to see where prices are higher in one country compared with Britain.	• A single currency could lead to a single political unit and the European Parliament making decisions currently made by the British Parliament. Britain will no longer be in charge of its own destiny.
• Retailers in all countries will be forced to reduce prices as they can be easily compared.	• A single interest rate will prevent a country setting its own interest rates to suit its own economic situation.
• A single currency will provide the same interest rate in all EU countries leading to economic stability.	
• A single currency will bind countries closer together ensuring peace rather than conflict in Europe.	

2.4 No longer three worlds

How has the collapse of communism changed patterns of development?

How might this affect the European Union?

A new economic order

While the European Union was developing, the USSR (*Union of Soviet Socialist Republics*) was competing with the USA to be the world's largest superpower. By 1989, however, it was clear that Soviet **communism** was not working. With the economy in ruins, President Mikhail Gorbachev agreed that individual republics could manage their own economies.

A

In 1973: textbooks referred to the Three Worlds

Key
■ The Third World

Tropic of Cancer
Equator
Tropic of Capricorn

Some former republics such as Estonia, Latvia and Lithuania (*The Baltic States*) became independent. They wanted to develop their economies by joining existing trade groups based on **capitalism**, such as the EU. Others formed the *Commonwealth of Independent States* (CIS) so that they could continue to work together. However this has not worked and the CIS no longer exists. These countries are now independent and known as the *Newly Independent States* (NIS).

What is the Third World?

The countries of the world can be divided into three groups. Two of these groups contain those countries where most people have a reasonable standard of living. These are usually regarded as the rich and developed countries. One of these groups includes the United States, Canada, Australia and the countries of Northern Europe. The other group contains the communist countries of Eastern Europe. These are the most powerful groups of countries that are sometimes called the major *power blocs*.

The third group is called the Third World. It contains those countries whose people suffer hunger and widespread sickness. In this group are the poorest countries of the world. These countries are struggling to develop better conditions. Until recently most of these countries were *colonies* of the wealthier nations

Source: The Third World, Roger Clare, 1973

B *A baseline for progress in the twenty-first century?*

The Newly Independent States (NIS) of the former Soviet Union						
Newly Independent States	Population (million)	Life expectancy (years)	GNP per person ($)	Primary workers (%)	Daily calorie supply (per person)	HDI Rank (out of 174)
Armenia	3.5	71	460	26	2 147	87
Azerbaijan	7.7	70	480	32	2 139	103
Belarus	10.3	68	2 180	20	3 101	60
Georgia	5.1	73	970	12	2 184	85
Kazakhstan	16.3	68	350	23	3 007	76
Kyrgyzstan	4.7	68	380	32	2 489	97
Moldova	4.3	68	380	32	2 562	104
Uzbekistan	23.9	68	950	42	N/A	92
Russia	147.2	67	2 260	14	2 704	71
Tajikistan	6.1	67	370	43	2 129	108
Turkmenistan	4.4	66	650	42	2 563	96
Ukraine	50.6	69	980	18	2 753	91
*Estonia	1.4	69	3 360	16	3 004	54
*Latvia	2.4	69	3 560	18	2 861	74
*Lithuania	3.7	70	2 540	22	2 805	62
NIS	**291.6**	**69**	**1 325**	**26**	**2 603**	**54 to 108**
EU-15	**380**	**80**	**23 499**	**5**	**3 415**	**5 to 28**

* The Baltic States are now classified with Central and Eastern European Countries (CEEC)
Sources: The World Guide 2001, Eurostat 2000, The World Bank website

The Newly Independent States (NIS) of the former Soviet Union

The way forward – join the EU?

Many *Central and Eastern European Countries* (CEEC) have decided that their future economic development lies in joining the EU. If the EU grows and poorer countries are seen to progress, this may encourage applications from the Newly Independent States (NIS). Their economic progress is well behind that of EU member countries. Existing EU members have mixed views on accepting new applications.

Key

- Present EU members
- First wave join 2004
- Second wave join later

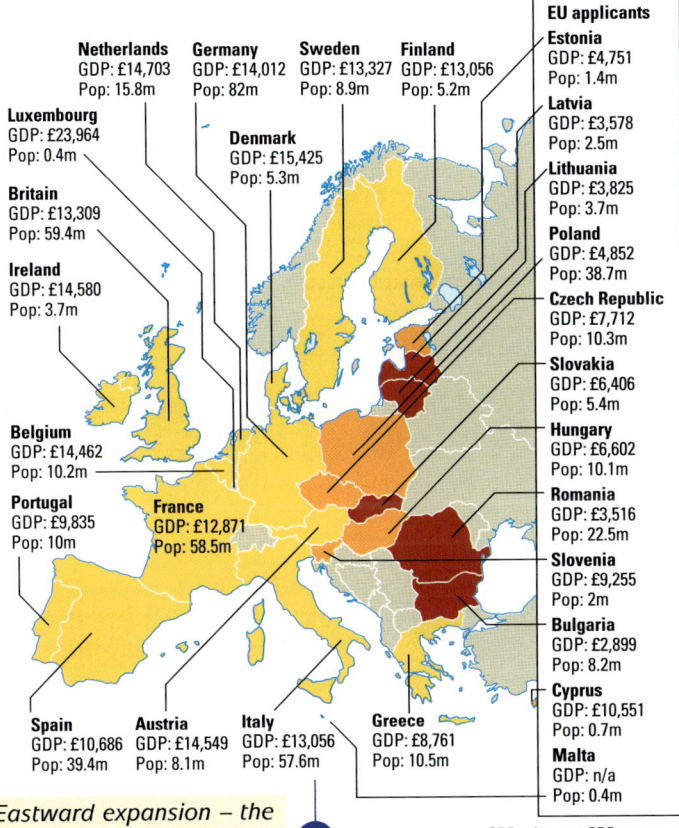

EU applicants

Estonia
GDP: £4,751
Pop: 1.4m

Latvia
GDP: £3,578
Pop: 2.5m

Lithuania
GDP: £3,825
Pop: 3.7m

Poland
GDP: £4,852
Pop: 38.7m

Czech Republic
GDP: £7,712
Pop: 10.3m

Slovakia
GDP: £6,406
Pop: 5.4m

Hungary
GDP: £6,602
Pop: 10.1m

Romania
GDP: £3,516
Pop: 22.5m

Slovenia
GDP: £9,255
Pop: 2m

Bulgaria
GDP: £2,899
Pop: 8.2m

Cyprus
GDP: £10,551
Pop: 0.7m

Malta
GDP: n/a
Pop: 0.4m

Netherlands
GDP: £14,703
Pop: 15.8m

Germany
GDP: £14,012
Pop: 82m

Sweden
GDP: £13,327
Pop: 8.9m

Finland
GDP: £13,056
Pop: 5.2m

Luxembourg
GDP: £23,964
Pop: 0.4m

Denmark
GDP: £15,425
Pop: 5.3m

Britain
GDP: £13,309
Pop: 59.4m

Ireland
GDP: £14,580
Pop: 3.7m

Belgium
GDP: £14,462
Pop: 10.2m

Portugal
GDP: £9,835
Pop: 10m

France
GDP: £12,871
Pop: 58.5m

Spain
GDP: £10,686
Pop: 39.4m

Austria
GDP: £14,549
Pop: 8.1m

Italy
GDP: £13,056
Pop: 57.6m

Greece
GDP: £8,761
Pop: 10.5m

Eastward expansion – the first and second waves. **C**

GDP = Average GDP per person

Are they good enough? Data for the first wave in 2004 **D**

Country	Population (million)	GDP per person (£)	Primary (%)	Secondary (%)	Tertiary (%)	HDI Rank out of 174
Estonia	1.4	4 751	16	32	52	54
Poland	38.7	4 852	28	36	36	44
Czech Republic	10.3	7 712	11	45	44	36
Hungary	10.1	6 602	15	38	47	47
Slovenia	2.0	9 255	6	46	48	33
Cyprus	0.7	10 551	14	30	56	26
The six applicants	53.1	7 287	15	38	47	26 to 54
EU-15	380	18 079	5	30	65	5 to 28

Farmers fear ruin from EU expansion east **E**

FARMERS FEAR RUIN FROM EU EXPANSION EAST

The future looks bleak for Maurice Demichel, a cattle farmer in France's sparsely populated Massif Central. In past years he has been given thousands of pounds in EU subsidies to stay in business producing beef. The EU is now preparing for former communist countries of central and eastern Europe to join in 2004. These countries have ten million poor farmers; there are eight million farmers in the existing EU.

Brussels now wants to cut subsidies to existing farmers; the money saved can then be given to help countries like Poland instead. Many existing farms will go out of business. 'If we argued with twelve countries and it got worse with fifteen, how on earth will we ever agree on anything with twenty-one countries?' said M.Demichel. The cuts also include reducing subsidies for milk and grain. Instead farmers will be paid a lower direct payment from the EU for their produce.

1
a The UK economy is mainly based on capitalism. Find out what the word capitalism means.
b How is communism different ?

2 Read **Source A**.
a Explain how the Third World was different from the other two worlds.
b Suggest why the terms MEDC and LEDC are now used.

3 Study **Source B**.
a Choose **one** country which you think is the most developed, and **one** country which you think is the least developed. Justify your choices.
b Many people in the UK do not know much about the Newly Independent States (NIS). Choose **one** country and write a short article of 50 to 100 words entitled 'Economic and social well-being in (your choice of country)'. Use an atlas, statistics in **Source B** and other reference sources to help.

4 Study **Source C**.
a What is meant by GDP per person?
b List the EU member countries in 2001 in rank order of GDP per person (1 = highest, 15 = lowest).
c Which six countries wish to join in 2004?

5 Study **Source D**.
a Which country would you consider:
• the most developed
• the least developed?
Justify your choices.
b How do these six countries compare with the EU countries?

6 Study **Source E**. To what extent do you agree with M. Demichel regarding new applicants from central and eastern Europe?

2.5 Questioning the Brandt Line

How did the Brandt report divide the world?
How relevant is the MEDC/LEDC division in the twenty-first century?

Simple and effective but relevant?

The Brandt Report (1980) has been very influential in the way that the world has been perceived. For over twenty years people have referred to the 'North-South' divide. The terms MEDC (The 'North') and LEDC ('The South') were used to refer to countries 'above' and 'below' the Line. Having a simple division has been very helpful but it can be misleading. Many so-called LEDCs have made progress and there have been major changes in global power blocs since 1980. How relevant is the Brandt Line in classifying development in the early years of the twenty-first century?

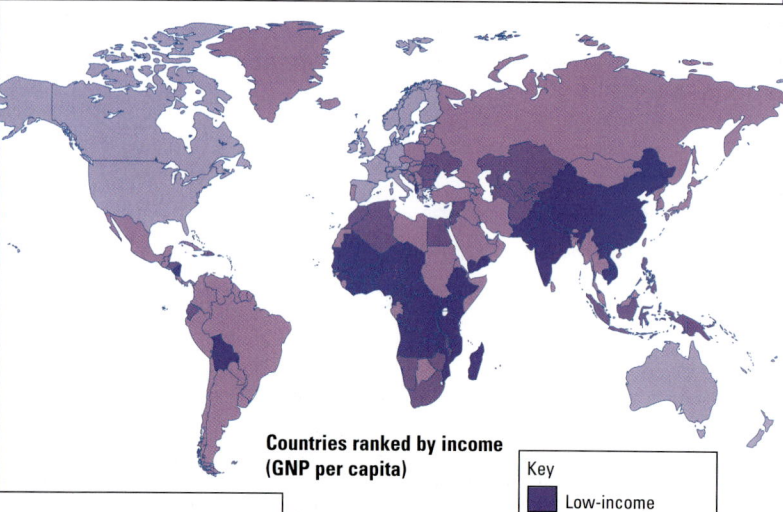

The world according to the World Bank in the year 2000 B

Countries ranked by income (GNP per capita)

Key
- Low-income economies
- Middle-income economies
- Upper middle-income economies
- High-income economies

Pan World Affairs

NORTH-SOUTH: A PROGRAMME FOR SURVIVAL
The Report of the Independent Commission on International Development Issues under the Chairmanship of Willy Brandt

There are obvious objections to a simplified view of the world as being divided into two camps. The 'North' includes two rich industrialized countries south of the Equator; Australia and New Zealand. The 'South' ranges from a booming, half-industrialized nation like Brazil to poor landlocked or island countries such as Chad or the Maldives. A few southern countries, mostly oil exporters, have higher per capita income than some of the northern countries. But in general terms 'North' and 'South' are broadly synonymous to 'rich' and 'poor', 'developed' and 'developing'.

Willy Brandt, 1980

A *The North-South divide*

C *The Human Development Index (HDI)*

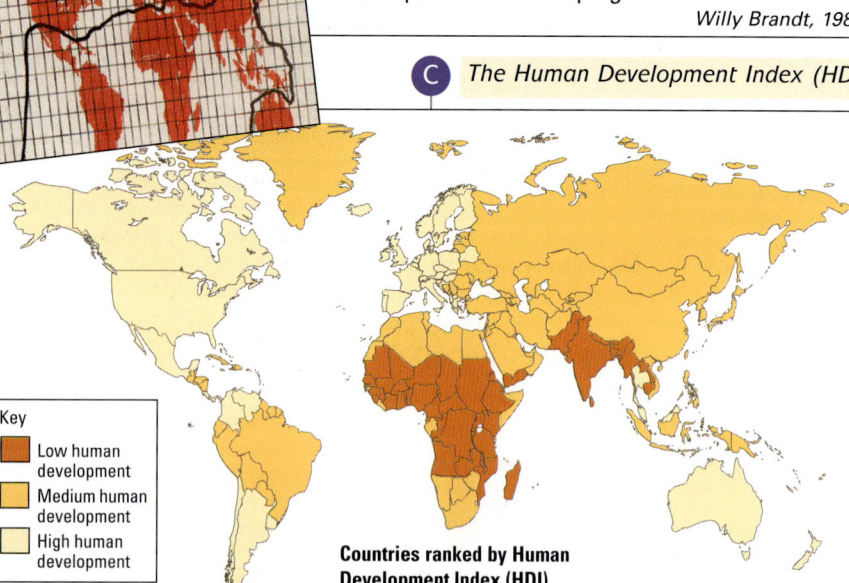

Key
- Low human development
- Medium human development
- High human development

Countries ranked by Human Development Index (HDI)

The top four	Index	The bottom four	Index
1 Canada	0.932	171 Burkina Faso	0.304
2 Norway	0.927	172 Ethiopia	0.298
3 USA	0.927	173 Niger	0.298
4 Japan	0.924	174 Sierra Leone	0.254

The HDI value is calculated by the United Nations Development Programme (UNDP) for the 174 countries in the world. It indicates how far a country has to go to attain certain goals: an average life span of 85 years, access to education for all and a decent income. The index ranges from 0 (least development) to 1 (highest development). The UK is ranked 10th with an index of 0.918.

1 Study **Source A**.
a What evidence is there that Brandt knew the 'North-South' divide was not perfect?
b Brandt still thought it helpful to draw the Line and divide countries into MEDCs and LEDCs. What do you think?

2 Study **Source B**.
a What is meant by GNP per capita?
b Why does the World Bank use it as a measure of development?
c Describe the distribution of the high-income economies.
d Compare this with the distribution of low-income economies.
e Refer to page 16. How well does the Brandt Line division work on this map?

3 Use an atlas together with **Sources B** and **C** to suggest **two** countries that:
- fit the Brandt division well.
- do not fit the division well.
Justify your choices.

Progress in Argentina

The *Brandt Report* identified three continents containing LEDCs. These were South-East Asia, Africa and South America. However, since 1980, many of these countries have made economic progress. A new classification could decide that some countries may be re-defined as MEDCs. A number of these are in South America.

D

Where is Argentina?

Country*	GNP per person $	Access to safe water %	Children per woman	Primary industry %	Secondary industry %	Tertiary industry %	HDI Ranking out of 174	Life expectancy (years)
Argentina	8 030	71	2.6	12	32	56	39	73
Bolivia	1 010	80	4.3	47	18	35	112	62
Brazil	4 630	76	2.3	23	23	54	79	67
Chile	4 990	91	2.4	18	26	56	34	75
Colombia	2 470	85	2.8	27	23	50	57	71
Ecuador	1 520	68	3.1	33	19	48	72	70
Guyana	780	91	2.3	22	25	53	99	65
Paraguay	1 760	60	4.1	39	22	39	84	70
Peru	2 440	67	2.9	28	20	52	80	68
Surinam	1 660	90	2.2	21	18	61	64	70
Uruguay	6 070	80	2.4	14	27	59	40	74
Venezuela	3 530	79	3.0	12	27	61	48	72
UK	21 410	99	1.7	2	29	69	10	77

Individual data not available for the separate French colony of French Guiana
Data from The World Guide 2001/2002 Oxfam, The World Bank website

E

Selected indicators for twelve countries of South America and the UK (1999)

Since 1990 the Argentinian government has sold many of its state economic activities to private investors many of which are based in MEDCs. Progress since then has been remarkable.

Population: of the 36 million people, 88 per cent of the population live in urban areas, with half in Buenos Aires. Most are white, mainly of Spanish and Italian descent. The official religion is Roman Catholicism.

Agriculture: the main industries are related to agricultural products. Grain and oilseeds are harvested and there are huge herds of cattle and sheep on the Pampas. Many farm-owners have converted buildings for tourists who can enjoy horse riding and helping on the farm.

Cattle ranching on the Pampas

Trade and industry: the economy used to rely on farm products e.g. tinned beef, but in 2000 the value of other manufactured goods exported was greater. Since diplomatic relations were restored with the UK after the Falklands conflict of 1982, UK companies are heavily involved in Argentina. GKN, BAT, BP, and Shell have bases there as well as British banks.

Services: Buenos Aires has become the most efficient port in South America. Costs are low and loading/unloading is quick. Airports are being upgraded to cope with increased tourism.

Tourism: with over five million visitors earning the country $5.5 billion a year this is the major growth industry. Buenos Aires is the most popular destination, followed by the Iguazo waterfall. The high peaks are ideal for mountain-climbing and trekking. The coasts have beaches and hotels. There are also modern winter ski resorts, which attract skiers from all over the world between June and September. Cruise ships bring money to the south coasts near Tierra del Fuego.

F

What's new in Argentina?

Energy: since 1990 Argentina's electricity industry has been run by foreign investment. The National Grid of the UK is a shareholder in Transener, the biggest electricity firm in the country. Any surplus is exported to Chile, Brazil and Uruguay. Natural gas fields are large and provide 45 per cent of the country's energy.

4 Study **Source D**.
a Describe the location of Argentina.
b Suggest **one** advantage that Argentina has for developing its economy when compared with Bolivia.

5 Study **Source E**.
a Name the countries of South America with the highest and lowest:
 • GNP per person • access to safe water
 • life expectancy • primary industry workforce
 • HDI ranking.

b Draw graphs to compare the data for Argentina with that of the UK.

6 Using the sources on this page, and other research, produce an illustrated A3 poster with the title 'Progress in Argentina since 1990.

7 'Argentina could be classified as a More Economically Developed Country; no other country in South America could.' Do you agree with this statement? Use evidence from **Sources E** and **F** to support your views.

Development, trade and aid

What is poverty?
How does poverty affect people?

2.6 Poverty – a world-wide perspective

Money doesn't matter?

Most people think of poverty as not having enough money. For many people it is more than just a lack of money. Poverty is the result of a complex mixture of factors.

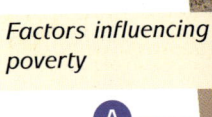

Factors influencing poverty

A

'Wealth is the blanket we wear. Poverty is to have that blanket taken away.' NGO member from Botswana

'Poverty is the squatter mother whose hut has been torn down by government for reasons she cannot understand.' Slum dweller from the Philippines

B

Poverty can be more than just a matter of money

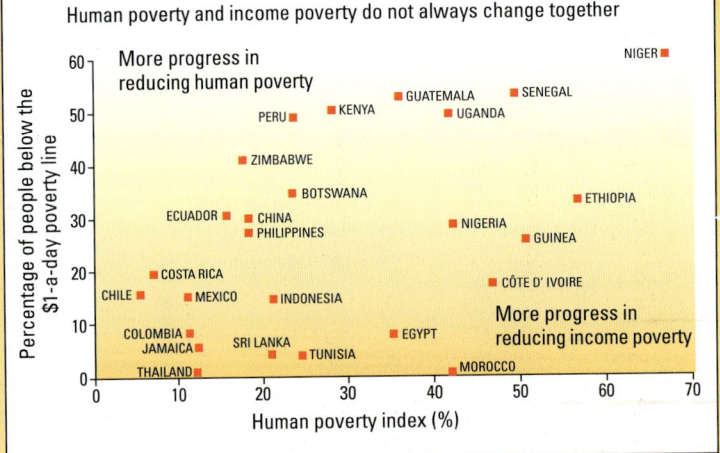

Human poverty and income poverty do not always change together

More progress in reducing human poverty

Percentage of people below the $1-a-day poverty line

NIGER
GUATEMALA SENEGAL
PERU KENYA UGANDA
ZIMBABWE
BOTSWANA
ECUADOR CHINA NIGERIA ETHIOPIA
PHILIPPINES GUINEA
COSTA RICA CÔTE D' IVOIRE
CHILE MEXICO INDONESIA
COLOMBIA More progress in
JAMAICA SRI LANKA EGYPT reducing income poverty
THAILAND TUNISIA
MOROCCO

Human poverty index (%)

Source: Human Development Report (most recent data)

'Poverty means never having quite enough to eat.' Panhandler from the USA

'Poverty is hunger, loneliness, nowhere to go when the day is over, deprivation, discrimination, abuse and illiteracy.' A single mother from Guyana

'Human poverty is much more than income poverty – it is the denial of choices and opportunities for living a tolerable life.'

---

1 Look at **Source A**.
   a Describe the scenes in the photos.
   b How does each photo show a form of poverty?
   c Suggest other forms of poverty which are not related to low income.

2 Read the quotes in **Source B**.
   a Make a list of evidence that poverty is:
      • related to a lack of money
      • related to other human factors.
   b Write your own definition of poverty. Explain your definition.

3 a Use **Source C** to place the countries in rank order according to the standard of living indicators.
   b Explain any difficulties you had with this task.

C *Selected standard of living indicators for five countries*

	UK	France	India	Burundi	Mexico
Personal computers per thousand	263	208	3	N/A	47
Televisions per thousand	645	601	69	4	261
Mains telephone lines per thousand	557	570	22	3	104
Infant mortality per thousand live births	6	5	70	118	30
Electricity used per person (KwH)	5241	6060	363	N/A	1459

Source: World Development Report 2000/2001

Juleka has only three possessions in the whole world. So why is she smiling?

She is smiling because she can operate a sewing-machine and because she is learning to read. Because her children are going to school and because for the first time in her life Juleka is beginning to gain confidence in her own abilities.

Deserted by her husband, Juleka lives with her three children in one of the poorest areas of Dhaka, Bangladesh. All she owns are her clothes and a cooking pot.

E

An advert from Concern Worldwide

 D

East Asia: poverty profile

- **Rural areas** have a substantially higher incidence of poverty than urban areas - in Indonesia, the Philippines, Vietnam and Laos, poverty is twice as high in rural areas compared with urban areas.

- **Regional variations** are also significant. For example, in Vietnam in 1993, poverty varied from 33.7% in the south-east of the country to 77.2% in the north-central part.

- There is a strong link between **education** and poverty throughout the region - lower education reduces earnings and increases vulnerability to poverty. This reduces a household's ability to educate its children.

- **Agricultural households** face a higher risk of poverty than any other group, with the percentage of poor people who live in agricultural households correspondingly high - 60% in the Philippines and 76% in Thailand and Vietnam.

- **Ethnicity** can be linked to poverty in certain countries in the region, such as Vietnam where poverty is substantially higher among some ethnic minorities.

Source: World Bank Group report 1998

4 Look at **Source D**.
  a Describe the main influences on poverty suggested by the report.
  b Suggest how each influence:
  • might help create poverty
  • could be challenged.

5 Look at **Source E**.
  a Compare Juleka's possessions with your own.
  b Suggest whether you or Juleka have a better
  • quality of life
  • standard of living
  Justify your views.

6 Look at the image of each country in **Source F**. To what extent does it reinforce the idea you gained from the standard of living indicators in **Source C**? Explain your response.

7 a Draw a web/spider diagram to show those factors that influence your own quality of life. Provide as much detail as you can and create links between different parts of your web.
  b Do you think quality of life is more or less important than standard of living? Explain your choice.

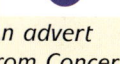
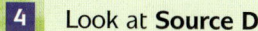

 F

Country images

2.7 Women and equality

Some are more equal than others

It is possible to measure differences between the lives of men and women for individual countries. This may be done by comparing indicators such as life expectancy, educational opportunities and income. Some clear worldwide patterns emerge.

Information about women's lives

MATTERS OF FACT

Women's Lives. On average, women in the least developed countries live **27 years** less than women in the industrialized world. Women in France and Japan live 83 years on average; the **life expectancy** of a woman in Sierra Leone is 39 years.  The average age at **marriage** for a woman in Mali or Niger is 16; in Japan, New Zealand and Singapore, it's 27. In Senegal, women spend about 2.5 hours a day gathering **wood for fuel**. In nearly every country, women work more hours than men – when paid and unpaid **labour** is taken into account. The global **average wage** for women is about three-fourths of the male wage – ranging from 92% of the male wage in Tanzania to 75% in Belgium, Germany and the US, to 42% in Bangladesh. In many African countries, women contribute up to 80% of the total **food production**, yet receive less than 10% of the credit to small farmers. In Latin America and the Caribbean, 85% of women can read and write; the **female literacy** rate in South Asia is 34%; in the Arab States, 41%. Every year, about one million children, mostly girls in Asia, are forced into **prostitution**. Of the 1.3 billion people living in **extreme poverty**, about 70% are women. Although women constitute half the electorate, they hold only 13% of the seats in the world's **parliaments**.

Information is drawn from the 1995 and the 1997 Human Development Reports, commissioned by the United Nations Development Programme. The reports are published in English by Oxford University Press and in other language editions by a variety of publishers.

In 1998, only 8 per cent of the world's cabinet ministers were women. *World's Women 2000, UN*	Two-thirds of school age children in the developing world without access to education are girls. *World's Women 2000, UN*	Globally, one woman dies of a problem related to pregnancy every minute. *The World's Women 1995: Trends and Statistics*	Women work two-thirds of the world's working hours, produce half the world's food, and yet earn only 10 per cent of the world's income and own less than 1 per cent of the world's property. *World Development Indicators 1997*

1
a What do you understand by inequality between men and women?
b Suggest reasons why it exists.

2 Study **Source A**.
a Make a list of ways in which women are treated differently from men.
b Identify and mark those that are:
  • related to income
  • related to other factors.

Facing the challenge

Three steps to self-help

- Little can be done to tackle women's poverty until working in the informal sector is recognized as being important to a country's economy.
- When people are recognized as being important, others take notice of them.
- When these other people begin to take notice, it is then possible to bargain and make demands aimed at improving the lifestyles of the country's informal workers.

SEWA

1 Paid maternity leave of 15 weeks

2 1 kg of protein-rich ghee (clarified butter) to build up the strength of the mother and child

3 Low interest rates on loans

4 Training to help women work more productively

B Over 120 000 women now benefit from SEWA membership. 95 per cent of all loans are repaid.

SEWA (Self Employed Women's Association) was started by Ela Bhatt, a lawyer, in 1972. It represents '**headloaders**' the unofficial porters of the textile industry in Ahmedabad, India. Mrs Bhatt later chaired a national commission on self-employed women whose findings were incorporated in India's **Five-Year Plan**.

In Bangladesh there is much discrimination against women ...

Within middle-class society, though, things are changing. In Parliament just over 10% of the seats are reserved for women and similar figures have been set for judges, university lecturers, lawyers and teachers.

This is **positive discrimination** that goes beyond anything that has happened in the United Kingdom. By putting women in prominent positions in public life there are two effects. It acts as an incentive to other women to set targets for their own lives. It also encourages the setting up of plans to help some of the many women in need. If women share control and responsibility, there is a greater chance of helping all women ... eventually.

C Changes in Bangladesh

Kashmir Education Foundation

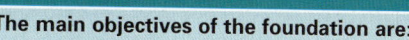

The main objectives of the foundation are:

To set up English medium schools and colleges in Pakistan and Azad Kashmir to provide quality education for girls and boys of poor families particularly from the backward and rural areas

To set up Teacher Training Institutes for female graduates particularly from rural areas to enable them to become quality English medium primary school teachers

To use the established schools and teacher training institutes as resource centres for replicating quality schools throughout the country

To upgrade the skills of teachers from other schools in the respective areas

D Improving educational opportunities

3
a Use the web in **Source B** to help you describe what SEWA offers to its members.
b Explain how each benefit will help to improve the life of an individual woman.
c How closely does SEWA support women along the 'three steps to self-help'?

4 Read **Source C**.
a Describe some of the challenges facing women in Bangladesh.
b Explain how the Bangladeshi Parliament is attempting to solve these problems.

5 Explain how the activities in **Sources C** and **D** help challenge gender inequalities.

6 Read what Ela Bhatt is saying in **Source E**. To what extent do you agree with her? Explain your response.

E Ela Bhatt

Whatever income goes into the hands of women, almost 98 per cent is spent on the family – for food, clothes, for the children's education, for shelter ... I strongly think that we should let more and more income go into the hands of women, so that the quality of life of the family will go up faster.

UNDP Choices, October 1997, page 13

2.8 Education or exploitation?

The importance of education

Education is regarded as a universal right and is used in calculating the Human Development Index. There is, however, a major mismatch between **adult literacy** rates in MEDCs and many LEDCs. While in most MEDCs almost all adults can read and write, the situation is very different in many LEDCs.

In LEDCs about 110 million children do not receive a primary education and about 275 million worldwide do not go to a secondary school. Statistics show that the situation is improving everywhere but at different rates. In the Arab States, for example, adult literacy improved from 30 per cent in 1970 to 57 per cent in 1995. During the same period, though, the rate in south Asia only rose from 32 per cent to 50 per cent.

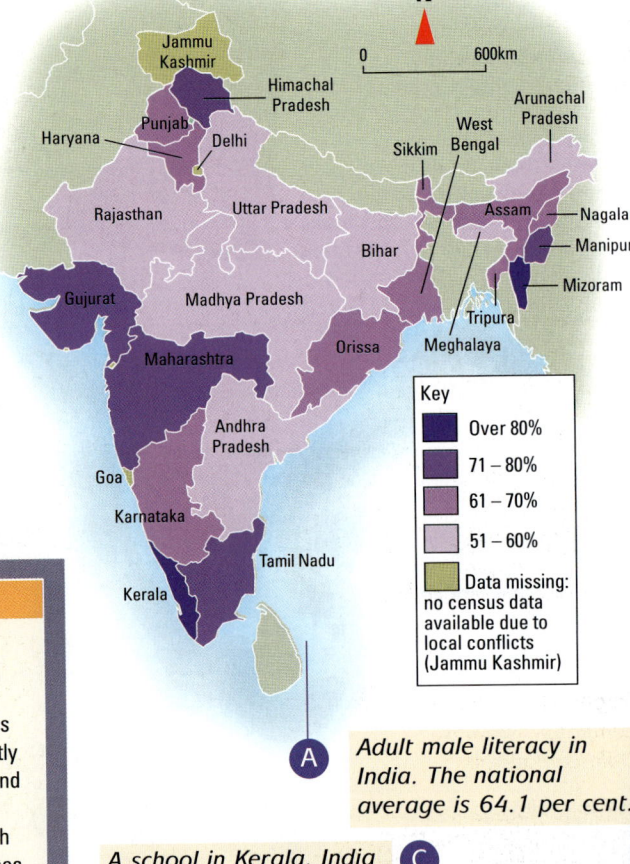

Key
- Over 80%
- 71 – 80%
- 61 – 70%
- 51 – 60%
- Data missing: no census data available due to local conflicts (Jammu Kashmir)

Adult male literacy in India. The national average is 64.1 per cent.

A school in Kerala, India C

Bajitpur Primary	
Fees	None
No. on roll	160
No. present	60
Buildings	None yet
Staff	5 untrained. All have other jobs. Spend most of time talking to each other.
Uniform	None
Teaching aids	Some pamphlet texts. No school furniture.

Nagla Natta Primary	
Fees	None
No. on roll	114
No. present	60 and rising
Buildings	3 brick and plaster rooms whitewashed walls. Partly funded by World Bank and partly by Uttar Pradesh.
Staff	3 full time teachers, each been on 2 training courses.
Uniform	None
Teaching aids	Teacher's desk, no other furniture yet. Blackboard.

*the exchange rate between £ sterling and Indian rupee is constantly changing. At the time of writing it was approx. Rs 67 to the £.

Information on three primary schools in Uttar Pradesh, India

B

Dr Sohan Singh Public School	
Fees	Rs 30 a month*
No. on roll	133
No. present	131
Buildings	3 room school house with a new room built each year. Privately funded.
Staff	3, all in same family that owns the school
Uniform	Maroon and white
Teaching aids	Wall charts and school desks. Pupils bring pens, satchels and exercise books.

1
a Describe what happened to adult literacy in the Arab States between 1970 and 1995.
b Compare this with changes in south Asia.

2 Study **Source A**.
a Describe the pattern of adult male literacy rates in India.
b Discuss why different countries and states in the same country could have different literacy rates.

3 Study **Source B**.
a Suggest which school is likely to be the most:
- successful
- unsuccessful
in terms of educating children. Explain your choices.
b Compare your 'first school' with that in **Source C**.

4 What is the value of education?

One alternative to school

Most young children in India are enrolled into school. Drop-out rates, though, are high and many children help their parents by working on the farm. Others work in factories, producing a huge variety of goods including footballs, trainers and rugs for sale in MEDCs.

Ashok, aged 11, was made to knot carpets from 6 a.m. until midnight and was not allowed to rest until the assigned work was completed even if it meant working all night. Once, when he fell asleep because he was tired, he woke up with a pain in his head and realized that the loom owner had hit him ... only when the bleeding did not stop was he taken to a doctor for the deep gash to be stitched. Since it was not feasible to shift another boy and teach him the design which Ashok was working on, the injured child was forced to work all night until the carpet was completed.

Source: Amnesty International.

Rugmark, an NGO, campaigns against child exploitation **E**

Rugmark works positively with employers to promote a product that does not exploit children. Employers commit themselves to:

- produce carpets without any illegal child labour involved;

- pay at least the minimum wages fixed by the government to their employees;

- provide a list of all their looms for unannounced inspection.

- Many loom sheds are poorly lit
- Wool dust is frequently inhaled
- Many children sleep next to the looms
- Danger from sharp knives used to cut the wool after each knot is made
- A hungry child stays awake longer
- Some employers physically and sexually abuse the children

There are over 300 000 child labourers in the Indian carpet industry **D**

5 Read the text on this page and look at **Source D**.
  a Describe the conditions for many children in the Indian carpet industry.
  b Suggest how each of the conditions described in **Source D** might affect the future health of the child.

6 Read **Source E**.
  a How does Rugmark aim to improve conditions in the carpet industry?
  b Explain why getting employers to agree to such changes might be more effective than trying to force them.

7 Discuss other ways in which children are exploited in both the UK and other countries. What are your views on such exploitation?

2.9 International trade

Africa and South America are missing out

Today the three most economically developed regions in the world are the USA, the countries of the European Union and the Asian **tiger economies**. These groups are increasing trade with each other. This is partly due to multi-national companies. Those based in the USA and EU are now locating in the Far East. Multi-nationals from the Far East are being attracted to develop bases in 'Western' countries. With China and India becoming major powers in the twenty-first century, east-west trading patterns may develop further, leaving a new 'north-south' divide similar to that identified by Brandt.

For many countries in Africa and South America, changing patterns of international trade may continue to keep them poor. Even though **globalization** by multi-nationals will provide some work, most profit will go back to the countries where they have their headquarters. To make economic progress, less economically developed countries may be left to develop their own economies, using aid and the expertise of **Non-Governmental Organizations (NGOs)**.

Trade in goods

A

Trade takes many forms

B Trade and trade barriers

Trade in services

The basic idea of world trade is that each country produces what it is best at producing and sells any surplus to other countries. With the foreign income from these exports the country can then buy what it needs. However, in recent years some LEDCs, using cheap labour, have been able to make goods cheaper than in some MEDCs. Textiles is a good example.

Protectionism can be used to restrict overseas goods by:
- introducing **tariff barriers**, for example adding import duties which increases the price, or limiting imports by **quotas** e.g. limiting the number of overseas cars that can be sold
- making laws on health and safety which keeps out overseas products not meeting these standards, e.g. fireworks
- implementing environmental regulations e.g. limits on vehicle pollution.

By keeping out overseas goods factories stay open, people can keep their jobs and the prices of home-produced goods can be kept up.

C *Some international trading blocs*

Regional bloc	Founded	Membership in 2000	World region
European Union (EU)	1957	France, Germany, Belgium, Luxembourg, Greece, Ireland, UK, Italy, Portugal, Spain, Denmark, Netherlands, Austria, Sweden, Finland	Western Europe
Organisation of Petroleum Exporting Countries (OPEC)	1960	Nigeria, Algeria, Tunisia, Libya, Saudi Arabia, Kuwait, Iran, Iraq, Yemen, Venezuela, UAE, Indonesia, Qatar	Africa, South America, the Far East and South-East Asia
Latin American Integration Association (LAIA)	1960	Argentina, Bolivia, Brazil, Chile, Colombia, Ecuador, Mexico, Paraguay, Peru, Uruguay, Venezuela	Central and South America
Association of South-East Asian Nations (ASEAN)	1967	Brunei, Indonesia, Malaysia, Philippines, Singapore, Thailand	South-East Asia
North American Free Trade Agreement (NAFTA)	1992	Canada, Mexico, USA	North and Central America

Since 1957 countries with common locations and economic interests have been joining together to make trade blocs. They provide a large total population as a market and can fix world prices for some products. Each group has a powerful regional influence on global trading patterns. A condition of joining any group, however, is that all countries must agree on the group's policy.

1 Study **Source A**.
  a What is meant by 'goods' and 'services'?
  b List the different methods used to transport goods between countries.
  c How is the transport of services different?

2 Study **Source B**.
  a List different ways in which countries protect their own industries.
  b Do you think 'protectionism' is more to the advantage of the producer or the consumer? Explain your view.

3 Study **Source C**.
  a On an outline world map shade in the trading blocs. (Note some countries belong to more than one trading bloc.)
  b Suggest why a country may want to belong to more than one trading bloc.
  c Give **one** advantage and **one** disadvantage for a country joining a trading bloc.

rade

is our closest daily link with people in poor countries. We buy everything from Indian shirts and Malaysian rubber to Colombian coffee and Caribbean bananas. One in three of our food products comes from the Third World.

Trade is a two-way process. If you cannot sell, you cannot buy. We rely on people from Peru to Fiji buying goods stamped 'Made in the UK'. So buying more from the Third World can help secure British jobs. Poor countries earn almost eight times more in trade than aid. They desperately need to sell more to lift their people out of poverty. But the present structure of world trade puts a lid on how much thay can sell. As a result the gap between rich and poor countries is getting wider. The richest 20% of the world's population creams off 80% of total world income. The poorest 20% gets less than 2%.

Extract from World Development Movement on trade

D

New photo

E Who gains from GATT and the WTO?

Queuing for water in Sierra leone...

'If we do this ... if we make it impossible for these 5.6 billion people to escape Coca Cola ... then we are sure of our future success for many years to come. Doing anything else is not an option.'

Coca Cola, Annual Report

Since 1947 there has been a **General Agreement on Tariffs and Trade (GATT)**. This has removed some trade barriers, such as tariffs and quotas, so that countries can operate **free trade** and compete more equally. Recently the **World Trade Organisation (WTO)** has replaced GATT and agreed:

• to make a 40 per cent reduction in global tariffs allowing fairer competition
• to reduce subsidies to farmers in Europe, the USA and Japan. This would make food prices rise in MEDCs so companies will look for cheaper food from LEDCs.

This would help LEDCs but in return they have to allow multi-national companies to locate in their countries. Three quarters of world trade is carried out by multi-national companies. World trade may be freer but it is not yet fairer.

In United Kingdom
15p UK VAT
3p shipping and processing
28p distribution
34p manufacturing and profit
5p other ingredients

In Cocoa Producing Countries
8p to cocoa farmer
7p transport, marketing and tax

Chocolate – who gets the biggest bite?

F

A few multi-national companies, including Mars, Nestlé and Cadbury-Schweppes, use over 80 per cent of the world cocoa. Raw cocoa beans are bought mainly from West Africa. Ghana grows much of the cocoa beans used in Britain. If they produce too much, or cocoa demand falls, the price they get paid falls. Ghana also makes chocolate but you cannot buy it in Britain because of tariffs that protect British producers. These make the price too high for imports

'It's all over for us unless there is a price rise soon ... nobody can afford to buy meat to eat, nor can we afford tools for clearing the ground around the crops. Our children are going without schoolbooks and old people in the village cannot afford to buy medicines.'

Cocoa farmer in Ghana

4 Study **Source D**.
a List the named products bought from LEDCs.
b How does the UK benefit from two-way trade?
c Why might increasing trade rather than giving aid be a better solution to economic development for LEDCs?

5 Study **Source E**.
a Write the quote from Coca Cola's Annual Report in your own words. What is your view of the statement?
b Suggest which of the WTO's agreements:
  • may help LEDCs increase their share of trade
  • hinders LEDCs increasing their share of trade.
  Explain your choices.

6 Study **Source F**.
a Which named multi-nationals are involved in producing chocolate?
b What percentage of the price of the chocolate bar goes to the cocoa farmer?
c Explain how demand for chocolate in MEDCs can affect the price received by the cocoa farmer.
d Suggest why chocolate made in Ghana is not sold in the UK. What is your view of this?

7 Read the cocoa farmer's comments in **Source F**. Draw an illustrated poster to show how different groups of people would suffer if the cocoa price went down.

2.10 Aid and fair trade can help

Changing overseas aid

In the past MEDCs have provided foreign aid to LEDCs. The **World Bank** and **International Monetary Fund (IMF)** have lent money so that LEDCs can build major projects from which all countries involved can benefit. This large-scale **traditional aid** is no longer thought effective. This is because:

- projects are often incomplete
- countries that cannot pay the money back stay in heavy debt
- the majority of people living in the country see little benefit.

Today the emphasis is on providing **intermediate aid** that helps people develop skills and become self-sufficient. Much of this work is carried out by Non-Governmental Organizations (NGOs) which have their main base in MEDCs. However, they have grass-roots contact through local officers based in LEDCs.

A *Many NGOs are providing intermediate aid*

I firmly believe that we need to be trained or helped to feed ourselves. It is only after one manages to win his daily bread that he can pursue other things. The way I look at this question is in line with one Chinese proverb which reads 'Give me fish and I will eat for a day, teach me how to fish and I eat for a lifetime'.

Ms Abebawork Abebe, Training Officer in Ethiopia for Japan International Co-operation Agency (JICA)

Money is not the first, but technicians and appropriate technology for the environment. If we are able to manage our existing resources properly, we can absorb grants for capital assistance.

Mr P.A. Kiriwandeniya, President SANASA (NGO) in Sri Lanka

IT brings hope to Rio's slums

Julio Santos, 15, used to hang around street corners in Rio de Janeiro. Now he vents his anger about the injustices of life in Rio de Janeiro's poverty-stricken **favelas** on the Internet. 'I am much better armed with computer skills. This way I may have a future,' he says.

Forty-six computer schools have been set up in the favelas of Rio de Janeiro

The clockwork radio does not need mains electricity or expensive batteries. All you do is wind it up for 20 seconds. This drives a dynamo that generates enough electricity to power the radio for 40 minutes. I thought of the radio after seeing a programme about the spread of Aids in Africa. Ignorance about the disease was down to a lack of communication. Many Africans could not afford to listen for information because of the high cost of batteries. With backing from the BBC World Service and the Overseas Development Agency, the radios are being sold to overseas aids organizations to be sold only to LEDCs.

Trevor Baylis with his invention the clockwork radio

REMOTE TRIBE GOES ONLINE

A tribe of 400 Brazilian Indians who inhabit a lush jungle reserve 100 miles south-west of Rio de Janeiro has become the first indigenous people of South America to enter the computer age. Although long suspicious of 'white men's habits' the Guarani Indians rejoiced at the arrival of PCs in their village. The PCs are a gift from the Committee for the Democratisation of Information, an NGO set up by Rodrigo Baggio.

It also set up the computer schools in Rio. 'There is still some way to go' said Rodrigo Baggio. 'The village needs electricity and phones before it can think of the Internet.' Chief Joao da Silva said 'We need to learn the technology of white men in our fight to keep and protect our lands, cultures and young people'.

Source: adapted from an article by Gabrielle Gamini in The Times Interface, 22 September 1999

Improving communications and technology **B**

1 Study **Source A**.
 a List the different NGOs shown. Add others to your list.
 b What do the two aid workers say is needed to help the countries in which they work?

2 Study **Source B**.
 a Suggest **three** ways in which computers and Internet access could benefit different groups of people in Rio de Janeiro.
 b What prompted Trevor Baylis to invent the clockwork radio?
 c Suggest benefits and drawbacks for people in remote LEDC villages from having access to:
 - computers and the Internet
 - the clockwork radio.
 Explain your answer.

In 1994 **The Body Shop** made an agreement to buy cocoa butter made from beans produced by organisations registered with the Max Havelaar Foundation whose mission is 'To represent and defend the integrity, rights and interests of small-scale producers in third world countries'.

Oxfam is well known for its clothing banks but it also helped to set up **Café Direct**. This organization enables many food producers to market their products in the UK and Ireland at a fair price for the growers.

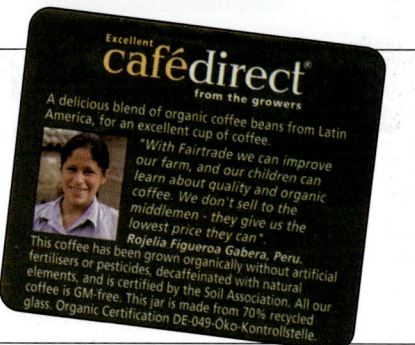

The Fairtrade mark goes on foods produced by independent growers and farmers in LEDCs. They cost a little extra to ensure that producers earn enough to look after their families. A Fairtrade label means the workers get:
• recognised trade unions
• no child labour
• decent working conditions
• a price that covers production
• an extra cost to improve conditions.

The Co-op now aims for every single Co-op brand product to be ethically sourced and sold for reasonable prices. It endeavours to ensure that the working and living conditions of the workers in LEDCs who produce Co-op products are decent.

 C *You can help too...*

 D *National and international aid targets*

The Department for International Development (DFID) is the government department responsible for managing Britain's programme of development assistance to poorer countries and for ensuring that government policies which affect developing countries, including the environment, trade, investment and agricultural policies, take account of developing country issues.

A number of international development targets to be reached by 2015 have been agreed by the United Nations. They include:

• primary education in all countries
• gaining equality for women women in education by 2005
• reducing child mortality rates by two-thirds and maternal mortality by three-quarters
• reproductive health services for all as soon as possible
• reversing current trends in the loss of environmental resources at both global and national levels.

 E *The debt issue*

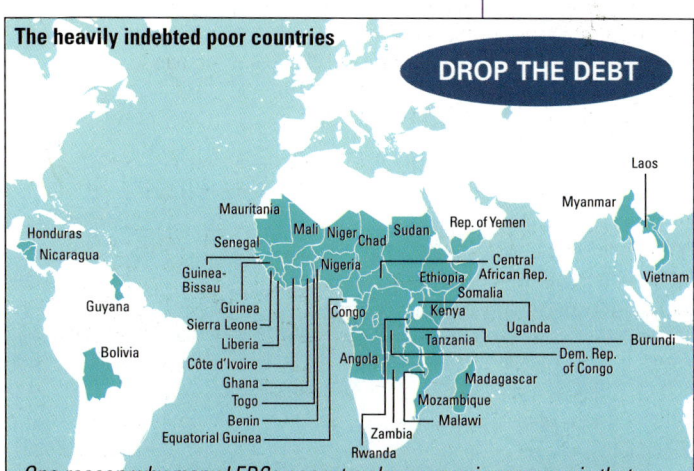

The heavily indebted poor countries

DROP THE DEBT

One reason why many LEDCs cannot make economic progress is that they owe money that has been lent to them over many years. For some there is little chance of paying it back. Some people think that MEDCs should cancel the debt and let these countries make a fresh start. But the debt is over $50 billion – a huge amount to be owed. In 1999 the UK cancelled one-third of the debt owed to it.

---

3 Study **Source C**.
a Describe how each example could help LEDCs increase their share of international trade.
b Add other examples of people or organizations raising money or giving aid to LEDCs that you are aware of or have taken part in.

4 Study **Source D**.
a What is the DFID? What does it do?
b What targets have been agreed by the United Nations?
c What is your view of these targets?

5 Study **Source E**.
a Describe the distribution of the heavily-indebted countries.
b To what extent might cancelling debt help the UN meet its targets?
c Would you cancel all of the debt? Explain your view.

6 Write a letter to the DFID suggesting ways in which different groups of people or organizations in the UK could help the UN achieve these targets.

2 It's the little things ...

A *The Village Platform*

The village of Balanfina (population 1 200), in southern Mali, is 30 miles from the nearest tarmac road. It can only be reached by foot or on a bumpy one-hour drive in a 4x4 vehicle. The villagers have to be self-sufficient. Since 1994, however, it has been linked to an electricity supply.

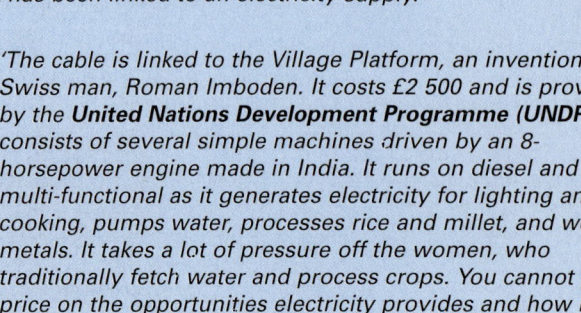

MALI

Balanfina

AFRICA

'The cable is linked to the Village Platform, an invention by a Swiss man, Roman Imboden. It costs £2 500 and is provided by the **United Nations Development Programme (UNDP)**. It consists of several simple machines driven by an 8-horsepower engine made in India. It runs on diesel and is multi-functional as it generates electricity for lighting and cooking, pumps water, processes rice and millet, and welds metals. It takes a lot of pressure off the women, who traditionally fetch water and process crops. You cannot put a price on the opportunities electricity provides and how it can improve the situation of women in Mali.'

Laurent Coche, UNDP worker

Small is beautiful?

Most people in the poorest LEDCs work in the primary sector. They spend much of their lives trying to grow food just to survive. To develop their economies and contribute more to international trade, these countries need resources to increase secondary and tertiary work opportunities.

One effective and sustainable way to change people's work patterns in less economically developed countries is to use money from wealthier countries to provide simple, cheap equipment. With training, the people can manage this equipment without help. This empowers them to change how they work and what they produce. They can then be responsible for their own decisions and development rather than rely on others.

'It has made our lives easier. The women can get their shea nuts ground in a machine instead of having to break them on a wall. We finish our work sooner so we can prepare dinner or help the men in the fields. We have time for a little gardening. If this makes our men happier then they will treat us better.'

Kani Sidibe, Head of Village Platform Management Committee

B *The Village Platform*

1 Study **Sources A** and **B**.
- a Who provided the Village Platform?
- b Describe how it works.

2
- a What impression is given about the role of men and women in Balanfina?
- b Explain how the Village Platform has changed the work of women in the village.
- c How do you think men feel about this? Suggest why.

3
- a Think of an invention that would improve the quality of life for people living in a village like Balanfina. It must be simple to operate, cheap and easy to mend if it breaks down. Explain your choice.
- b Plan it, cost it, make it and market it!

3

Economic activity

KEY IDEAS

The location of different economic activities is influenced by a range of factors.

National and multi-national companies have an increasing influence on employment opportunities and economic development?

Silicon Valley in California, USA has become the main headquarters for many companies involved in the ICT industry

3.1 Locating economic activity

Where should we locate?

The factors that influence the location of economic activities vary. Many primary industries, such as mining, must locate where the raw material being exploited is found. Likewise, some tertiary industries, such as tourism, often rely on natural or cultural features of an area for their growth. Many secondary industries, however, have no single locational influence. They will often weigh up the advantages and disadvantages of a number of locations before deciding where to build.

A Decisions, decisions...

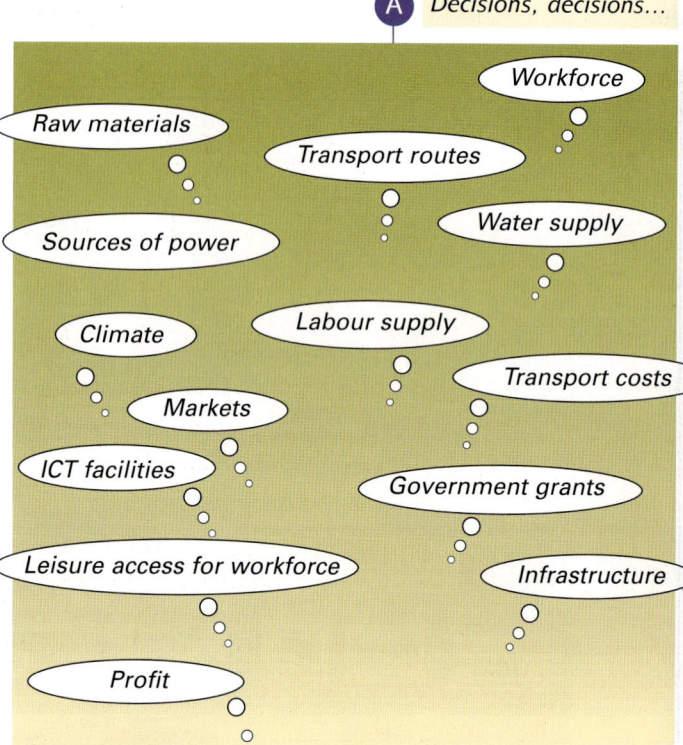

- Raw materials
- Workforce
- Transport routes
- Sources of power
- Water supply
- Climate
- Labour supply
- Markets
- Transport costs
- ICT facilities
- Government grants
- Leisure access for workforce
- Infrastructure
- Profit

B

The Annesley Bentinck Colliery closed in January 2000. It had been one of the few left in the Nottinghamshire Coalfield. Most shut down in the 1980s because of competition from imported coal that was subsidised by the governments of the producing countries .

C

Home Farm, Nottinghamshire is also an example of a primary economic activity. It is located where the land is suitable for several types of farming. The decision as to which type of farming to carry out is partly controlled by physical influences e.g. the climate, but also by human influences e.g. the availability of EU subsidies.

Newstead Abbey, once the home of Lord Byron, is visited by thousands of tourists each year. It is an example of a tertiary economic activity. The number of visitors it receives is influenced by the weather and the disposable income people have.

D

1 Explain how each factor in **Source A** may influence the decision as to where to locate a new economic activity.

2 a Give a six-figure grid reference for the location of the photograph from **Source E**.
b Suggest the locational factors that were responsible for the rise and fall of this industry in Nottinghamshire.

3 a Home Farm farmhouse is located at grid reference 501521 on **Source E**. Describe the site and situation of the farm.
b Suggest the locational factors that influence the use of land on this farm.

4 Study **Sources A–E**. How might factors influencing the location of a factory, be different to those influencing the location of:
- primary activities (the mine and the farm)
- tertiary activities (visitors to the Abbey)?

Site and situation

Most locational factors may be organised under the headings of site and situation. The site is characteristics of the land on which the industry is found. The situation is the relationship of the site to the area surrounding it. The Sherwood Business Park is a tertiary economic activity located close to Junction 27 of the M1 motorway in north Nottinghamshire.

Site of Sherwood Business Park:
- an area of regular shape, large enough for current use and expansion
- land that is flat
- provision of utilities such as electricity, water, telephone, and sewage disposal
- a pleasant park-like appearance.

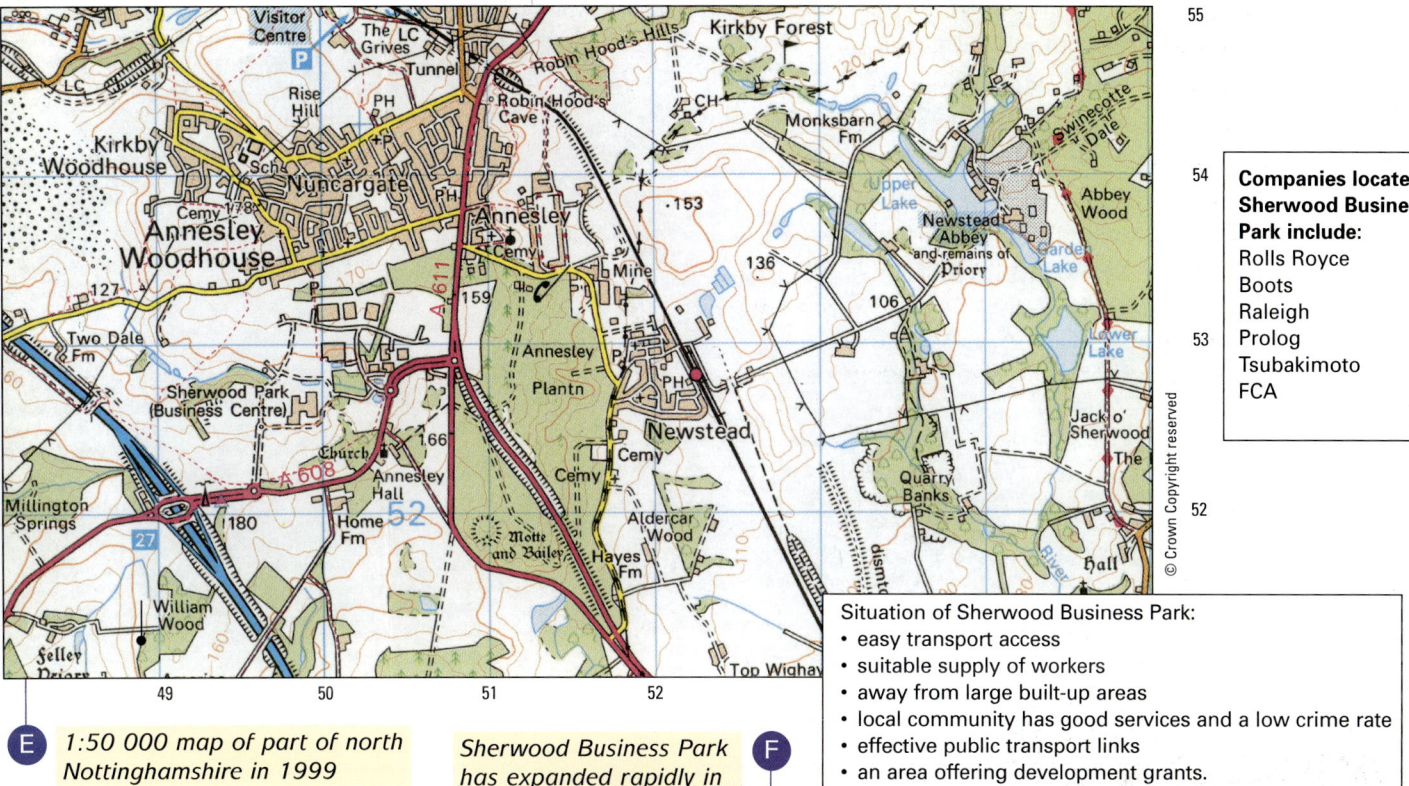

Companies located in Sherwood Business Park include:
Rolls Royce
Boots
Raleigh
Prolog
Tsubakimoto
FCA

E 1:50 000 map of part of north Nottinghamshire in 1999

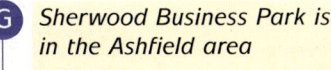

Sherwood Business Park has expanded rapidly in only a few years

Situation of Sherwood Business Park:
- easy transport access
- suitable supply of workers
- away from large built-up areas
- local community has good services and a low crime rate
- effective public transport links
- an area offering development grants.

G Sherwood Business Park is in the Ashfield area

Welcome to Ashfield!

Shaping up for the future – that's the message coming from this busy and exciting district, and there is certainly plenty to look forward to. Enjoying a prime location right in the heart of the Midlands, Ashfield is an area of interesting contrasts. It's an area that has a clear vision of creating a prosperous, dynamic, competitive economy with world-class business staffed by a skilled, motivated workforce and a community that enjoys health, safety and a green environment.

The District's choice location makes it the obvious choice for business – the M1 runs right through Ashfield, the East Midlands Airport is on its doorstep, and local stations link onto the national Intercity rail network.

Dozens of internationally known companies have already located in Ashfield – among them Rolls Royce, Kodak and Pretty Polly whose products are household names. The creation of the flagship Sherwood Business Park enterprise zone within Ashfield has given the district a further boost, with numerous new companies taking advantage of the ideally placed site.

5 On a sketch of **Source F**, use **Sources E** and **G** to help you:

a label the important site and situation features of the Sherwood Business Park

b annotate each feature to show how it may encourage businesses to locate on the 'park'.

6 To what extent do you think that the Sherwood Business Park is a good place to locate a tertiary economic activity?

3.2 Down on an EU farm

Plenty of food from few workers

In the UK agriculture remains an important primary industry. However, because of the increased use of machinery, only a small number of people still work on the land. In the year 2000 there were less than half a million farmers, under 2 per cent of the UK workforce.

Much of the food eaten by the other 98 per cent of the population is produced by these farmers. Their produce also brings in valuable export earnings.

Glebe Farm is an **arable** farm in East Lindsey, Lincolnshire. Bill Atkin has owned it since 1973. His father bought the farmhouse at Barley Cliff in 1946 and the land in 1960.

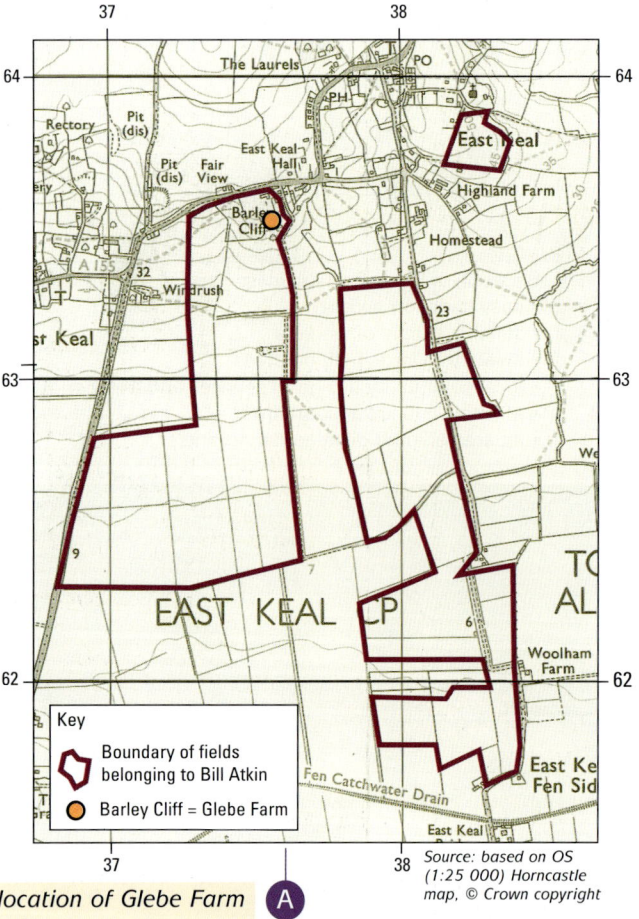

The location of Glebe Farm **A**

Source: based on OS (1:25 000) Horncastle map, © Crown copyright

Key
Boundary of fields belonging to Bill Atkin
Barley Cliff = Glebe Farm

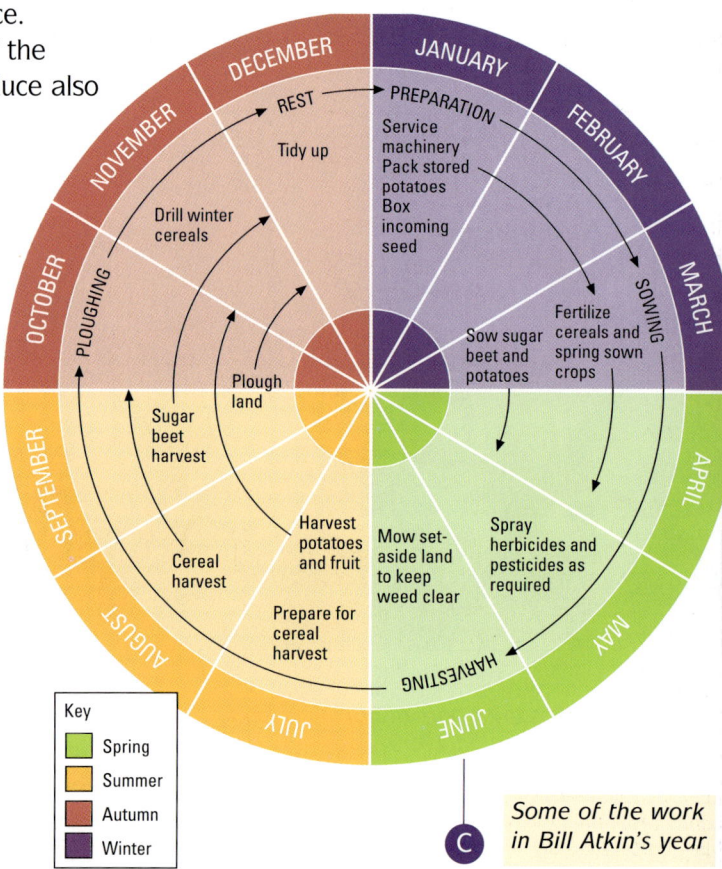

Some of the work in Bill Atkin's year **C**

Key
- Spring
- Summer
- Autumn
- Winter

'We get a long growing season here but, as we are in the east of England, the summers are rather dry. The soil is not damp enough all year to grow lush grass, so keeping cattle or sheep is not possible. I wouldn't want to get up and milk twice a day anyway. The farm faces south so the drier northern fields drain down into a flat fen which is wet. I plan the work so that the crops needing less attention are further away from the farm buildings. The sandy soil drains well and warms up quickly but I need to add fertilizers like NPK*. I use sprays to protect Brussels sprouts and cereals. Because acid rain has been reduced I now have to add a sulphur spray to remove powdery mildew.'

Bill Atkin

* NPK – a mix of Nitrogen-Phosphate-Potassium

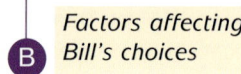

Factors affecting Bill's choices **B**

1 Study **Sources A** and **B**.
a Draw a labelled sketch map to show:
- Barley Cliff farmhouse
- the village of East Keal
- roads and drains
- the fields owned by Bill.

b Add labels around the map to show how physical factors influence farming here. (Refer to rainfall, temperature, aspect, soil, drainage.)

c How does Bill overcome any problems caused by these factors?

d Explain why Bill has continued arable rather than pastoral farming here.

2 Study **Source C**.
a From Bill's farming calendar list the main activity carried out in each season.

b Suggest advantages and disadvantages of working as a self-employed farmer compared with being employed as an office worker. Which would you prefer?

The influence of the EU

Since 1973 the **Common Agricultural Policy** of the EU has had a major influence on what farmers produce. Farmers can grow what they like on their own land but will only be paid grants and subsidies for meeting EU production targets. In the UK this has led to a reduction of wheat production and an increase in crops like oil-seed rape.

In recent years other grants have been given by the EU to set aside land for conservation and to keep public footpaths open. Farmers rely on these grants for their income. This has not only affected the farmer's choices but also changed the appearance of the rural environment of the UK.

'Since joining the EU my land use has been greatly affected. I have diversified greatly in the last 20 years. I grow strawberries on land near the road and have added raspberries. I also have a Caravan Club site for five caravans. Without these extra activities and EU grants and subsidies, farmers like me would be bankrupt. People just wouldn't pay the full price to cover costs. I've grown some linseed on a set-aside field since 1993. That way I get two EU grants: one for not growing wheat and one for growing linseed. I may also grow some rape. I take part in set-aside schemes concerned with conservation such as growing trees and increasing hedgerows and ponds for which I can claim grants. After all, it's in the farmer's interest to look after the countryside.'

Bill Atkin

D *The EU changes land use*

Land-use at Glebe Farm **E**

Field number	Area in hectares
2878	3.38
4451	1.41
3441A	0.26
3441B	3.72
5635A	3.62
5635B	1.00
5635C	0.63
5635D	1.77
5635E	0.76
5635F	0.86
3200	3.19
4400A	4.72
4400B	0.86
7000A	0.84
7000B	11.82
7000C	0.47
4748	2.15
0017	8.80
0003	7.94
0269A	5.29
0269B	3.17
2100	2.83
1753	4.80
0023	7.79
3322	4.04
1388	10.17
3600	3.06
2973	5.51
3346	5.47
0669	7.17
0545	9.23
TOTAL AREA 126.7 hectares	

Can Bill claim his EU Area Payment? **F**

Key

Wheat	Pasture
Sugar beet	Set-aside land
Potatoes	Farm buildings
Brussel sprouts	Road/yard
Peas	Trees
Strawberries (P.Y.O)	— Field boundary or drain
Raspberries (P.Y.O)	--- Field boundary (temporary)
	▬ Farm boundary

3 Study **Sources D** and **E**.

a How has Bill diversified his farm business in the last 20 years? Give reasons for this.

b Suggest advantages and disadvantages of diversification for a farmer.

c How have EU policies affected the land use and appearance of the rural environment of Bill's farm? What is your view of these changes?

4 Study **Sources E** and **F**.

To claim his EU Area Payment, Bill must show that he has set-aside 15 per cent of the land on which he would normally grow wheat. **Source F** shows the return he filled in for the numbered fields on **Source E**. To see if he qualified for his payment do the following calculations.

a Add up the total area of land used for:
 • wheat
 • set-aside land (field numbers 2878, 3441B, 5635A, 5635F)
 • the total for wheat and set-aside together.

b Calculate the percentage of the total that is just set-aside land.

c Has Bill done his calculations correctly?

5 'Interference in UK farming by the EU is not to the benefit of the farmer or the countryside.' To what extent do you agree with this statement?

41

3.3 At the crossroads of Europe

Key

— Oil pipeline under construction

···· Gas pipeline under construction

N

0   100km

RUSSIA

Black Sea

Tuapse

Samsun

GEORGIA   Tbilisi

TURKEY

Yerevan   ARMENIA   AZERBAIJAN   Baku

Caspian Sea

Pipeline from Turkmenistan

IRAN

A The crossroads of Europe

Baku city and port

C The EU gives a helping hand

 B *Azerbaijan – MEDC or LEDC?*

	Azerbaijan	UK (MEDC)	Sierra Leone (LEDC)
Population (millions)	7.7	58.7	4.7
GNP per head ($)	480	21 410	140
Children per woman	2.0	1.7	6
Life expectancy	70	77	38
Primary (%)	37	2	68
Secondary (%)	24	19	15
Tertiary (%)	39	79	17

Source: The World Guide 2001

A new beginning

Armenia, Georgia and Azerbaijan are three former republics of the Soviet Union. Together they are known as the Caucasus Republics, a name taken from their location in the Caucasus mountains. They are found where Europe meets Asia. This 'crossroads of Europe' has seen clashes between Christians and Muslims, resulting in a culturally rich but socially divided region.

With the loss of Soviet markets and low levels of economic development, these countries are relying on aid from MEDCs to improve their standard of living. Loans and assistance from the *International Monetary Fund* (IMF) and the *EU Technical Assistance to the CIS* **(TACIS)** scheme have helped the countries progress so that they rely less on foreign aid. Azerbaijan is also making economic progress because of its oil resources.

Tacis News

The global market economy is based now on the EU, the USA and the Far East. These countries are providing aid and technical assistance to former states of the USSR which contain many under-developed resources and a huge, but poor, population.

Millions of people would have been queueing in front of empty bakeries last winter if the EU had not stepped in to help the people of Armenia, Azerbaijan and Georgia. Surplus cereals from the EU helped overcome serious food shortages. TACIS used EU funding to mend railway lines in mountainous areas including those destroyed by the Armenian earthquake in 1988. In April 1996 Armenia, Azerbaijan and Georgia signed Partnership and Co-operation agreements (PCAs) with the European Union. These are a major step towards integrating these countries into the wider European economy.

1 Study **Source A**.
a Describe the location of Azerbaijan.
b What advantages does the location of Baku have for international trade both in and out of Azerbaijan?

2 Study **Source B**.
a Draw graphs to compare development indicators for the three countries shown.
b Rank the countries from *most* to *least* developed. Justify your rankings.
c 'Azerbaijan has more in common with an MEDC like the UK than an LEDC like Sierra Leone.' Discuss this statement.

3 Study **Source C**.
a Suggest why Azerbaijan needs outside aid.
b In what ways is the EU using its funds to help?
c Suggest why the EU is providing this aid. What is your view of this use of EU funds?

Drilling for oil – a changing location

Farming has been an essential primary activity for thousands of years but some natural resources still provide new opportunities for economic development. Extracting oil is a relatively recent activity. Oil companies are constantly carrying out exploration for new reserves.

In 1900 the Baku oil reserves were the most important in the world. The location of this activity then moved to other areas as new reserves were exploited. Present-day estimates show that the Azerbaijan reserves are second in quantity only to those of the Middle East. Many 'Western countries' do not want to rely only on Middle East oil because of past conflicts caused by political and religious differences. A new location in Central Europe for this primary resource would be attractive to large consumers such as the USA. There is every reason to believe that, based on oil exports, Azerbaijan could develop rapidly in the twenty-first century. However, once the oil runs out, will it be able to survive by selling other products?

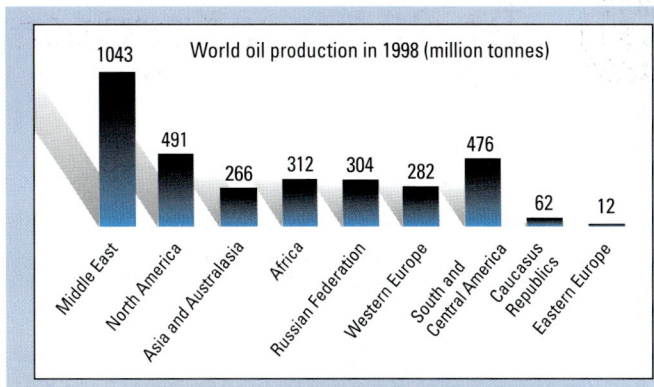

World oil production in 1998 (million tonnes)

World oil production and consumption 1998 **D**

In come the multi-nationals... **E**

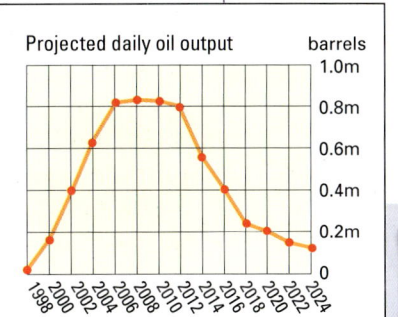

Projected daily oil output

World region	Consumption (million tonnes)
North America	935
Asia and Australasia	804
Western Europe	541
South and Central America	187
Middle East	144
Russian Federation	122
Africa	91
Eastern Europe	80
Caucasus Republics	50

Source: Oil and Gas Journal 2000

If you stand long enough in the foyer of the Baku headquarters of Socar, Azerbaijan's state oil company, you will see much of the world's oil industry pass by.

4 Study **Source D**.
a Which **two** regions dominated world oil production in 1998?
b Draw a bar graph to show world oil consumption by region.
c List regions that:
  • are *net importers*, i.e. consume more than they produce
  • are *net exporters*, i.e. produce more than they consume.
d Suggest why the USA has recently abandoned environmental policies in order to explore for more oil within its own country. What is your view?

5 Study **Source E**.
a Describe the predicted trends in oil production, 1998–2024.
b Describe how western companies such as BP have ensured they can exploit the oil without upsetting Russia
c Suggest why multi-national oil companies are keen to invest in oil exploration in Azerbaijan.
d Suggest how Azerbaijan should use its 'wall of money'.

6 Study **Source F**.
a List **two** multi-national companies from each of the primary, secondary and tertiary sectors.
b List goods or services associated with these companies.
c Suggest **two** advantages and **two** disadvantages of relying on multi-national companies to help economic and social progress.

7 Imagine you are part of a delegation in charge of attracting investment and aid into Azerbaijan to help economic progress. You have a stand at an international trade exhibition in London. Produce a short, illustrated presentation telling delegates about the country and its opportunities.

The Azeris await riches of Caspian oil bonanza

An avalanche of hard cash is about to descend on the Caucasian republic of Azerbaijan. Vast wealth will arrive almost overnight on this little-known region of the world. The Azeris call it 'the wall of money'.

The current boom is due to Western technology. The oil lies deep in the Caspian Sea. It is accessible by drilling techniques perfected in the North Sea. 'Western companies have done more in the past four years than the Soviet Union did in forty,' said one oil executive. The Russians tried to prevent Western companies such as BP drilling in the Caspian Sea, which is shared between the countries that border it. So the multi-nationals allowed Lukoil, Russia's main oil company, to take 100 000 barrels from Baku to the Russian Black Sea port of Novorossiysk. BP are also repairing an old pipeline between Baku and Supsa (Georgia) so that oil can be sent to the Black Sea and then by tanker to the Mediterranean Sea.

Source: Adapted from Michael Dynes, *The Times*, 5 May 1998

you won't be the first...

Agip, Amoco, British Petroleum/Statoil, British Telecom, Caterpillar, Chevron, Conoco, DHL, Dillingham Construction, Dresser Industries, Elf Aquitaine, Ericsson, Ernst & Young, Halliberton, Hewlett Packard, HSBC Gibbs, Honeywell, Itochu, John Laing, KPMG, Kvaerner, Leica AG, Lufthansa, Manitou, McDermott, Mobil, Morrison International, Motorola, Olivetti, Pennzoil, Price Waterhouse, Racal, Ramco, Raychem, Sedgewick Insurance, Shell, Siemens, Sun Microsystems, Texaco

F

...to do business in Azerbaijan... don't be the last

You won't be the first

3.4 The UK relies on inward investment

How successful has the UK been in attracting inward investment from overseas?

Is giving aid for inward investment fair?

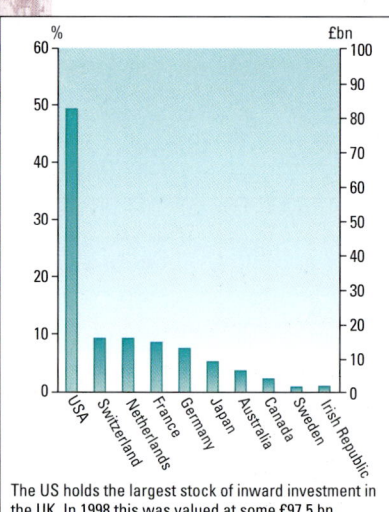

The US holds the largest stock of inward investment in the UK. In 1998 this was valued at some £97.5 bn, representing 49% of total FDI in the UK.

FDI = Foreign Direct Investment

A *Foreign Direct Investment (FDI) in the UK in 1998*

B *Inward investment projects, 1999-2000*

Country	Projects	Total associated jobs
USA	363	67 991
Germany	63	8 982
Japan	58	11 401
Canada	48	10 390
France	47	14 639
Irish Republic	22	1 445
Sweden	19	1 873
Netherlands	17	1 875
Australia	13	1 280
South Africa	13	3 265
Rest of EU	41	4 000
Others	53	7 053
TOTAL	757	134 194

C *Investors from the east...*

Made in Britain – owned abroad

While primary industries, such as farming in the UK and mining in Azerbaijan, remain an important part of their economies, traditional secondary (manufacturing) industry has declined. Today much of the secondary activity taking place in the EU is controlled by **multi-national companies** from outside the EU. These companies are mainly based in the world's three largest individual economies, the USA, Japan and South Korea. They invested heavily in the UK in the 1990s and, although new investment has slowed down, these countries still favour the UK. This is partly because it provides access to the market of nearly 400 million people living in the European Union.

Regions that benefited from overseas investment during the 1990s **D**

Biggest Foreign Investors during the 1990s		
1	Daewoo Electronics	S. Korea
2	LG Electronics	S. Korea
3	Fujitzu	Japan
4	Siemens	German
5	Chunghwa	Taiwan
6	Sony	Japan
7	IBM	America
8	Compaq	America
9	Hyundai	S. Korea
10	Motorola	America
11	Michelin	French
12	Oki	Japan
13	NEC Semiconductors	Japan
14	AT&T	America
15	Digital	America
16	Samsung	S. Korea
17	Honda	Japan
18	Nissan	Japan
19	Toyota	Japan
20	Robert Bosch	German

*A multi-national company or trans-national company (TNC) has its headquarters in one country and at least one other branch in another country.

1 Study **Source A**.
  a Which country accounted for the largest inward investment into the UK in 1998?
  b What evidence suggests that EU and non-EU countries also invest in the UK?

2 Study **Source B**.
  a Which country accounted for:
    • the most projects in the UK during 1999-2000
    • the most jobs created?
  b Name examples of some companies from this country which have branches in the UK.

3 Study **Source C**.
  a Japan and South Korea are both tiger economies. Use the glossary to define 'tiger economy'.
  b What is the message of the cartoon?

4 Study **Source D**.
  a What is a multi-national company?
  b Copy and complete the table below. South Korea has been completed. Use **Source E** and additional research to complete the Products column.

Country where multi-national has its headquarters	Name of multi-national companies	UK Standard Regions	Example of product	Number of different multi-nationals from the same country
South Korea	Daewoo Elec. LG Electronics, Hyundai, Samsung	Northern Ireland South Wales Scotland North East	Electronics Semi-conductors Electronics Televisions	4

E. The Enterprise Centre of Europe: what Britain can offer

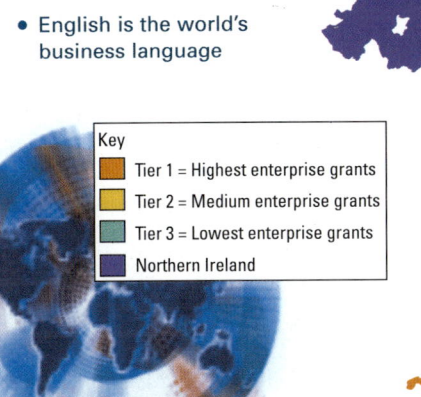

invest·uk key facts 2000

- A hard-working, educated and healthy workforce with days lost by strikes and sickness the lowest in EU
- A strong science, technology and communications base
- A market of 58 million consumers and access to the world's largest free trade area with nearly 400 million people in fifteen EU countries
- Quick toll-free motorways to air and sea ports
- Nowhere further than 100 miles (160km) from a container port
- The lowest energy costs in the EU
- London is Europe's business capital
- The lowest business tax rate in the EU
- The Channel Tunnel link
- English is the world's business language

Scotland

Northern Ireland

North East

North West

Yorkshire & Humberside

East Midlands

West Midlands

Wales

East Anglia

South West

South East

Key
- Tier 1 = Highest enterprise grants
- Tier 2 = Medium enterprise grants
- Tier 3 = Lowest enterprise grants
- Northern Ireland

invest·uk replaced the Invest in Britain Bureau (IBB) in 1998. The new Assisted Areas are similar to those where grants and incentives were available during the 1990s when the multi-nationals located in them as shown on **Source D**.

'The good news is that the United Kingdom is the place to do business electronically.'

Bill Gates, Financial Times, 3 November 1999

Country	Internet growth (%)	Months behind US
Netherlands	210	13
UK	280	11
Spain	185	35
Denmark	220	19
France	215	22
Germany	200	15
Norway	200	17
Finland	160	21
Italy	145	34
Sweden	170	7

F. ICT – the fastest growing market

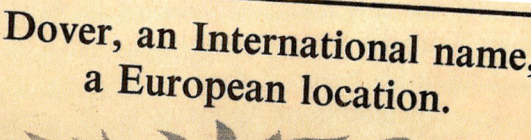

Dover, an International name, a European location.

DOVER

WHITE CLIFFS BUSINESS PARK DOVER

DOVER

The name Dover is known throughout the world, but many business leaders may not yet know that it is establishing itself as a quality business location with real benefits.

The area's strategic location is obvious, but consider the real benefits of operating from a flagship site in Dover; communications, low cost, grants, people, European market access, terrific lifestyle benefits and a civic determination to welcome and assist.

G. Dover – hub of the South

5 Study **Source E**.
a Describe the location of the closest Tier 1 area to where you live.
b What is the difference between Tier 1 and 3 enterprise grants?
c Describe the distribution of Assisted Areas in the UK.
d Compare this with the distribution of multi-national companies shown in **Source D**.
e Comment on your findings.

6 a Rewrite the countries in **Source F** in rank order of Internet growth in 1999.

b Which EU country had the:
  • fastest Internet growth
  • slowest Internet growth?
c What evidence from your table suggests that the UK is a good place for ICT companies to invest?

7 Study **Source G**.
a Many towns and cities are competing for new business from abroad. Dover is in an Assisted Area. Suggest some advantages for a new business locating near Dover.
b Devise a similar poster advertising your own area as a place of inward investment.

3.5 Welcome to Wales

Why did LG choose to locate in South Wales?

What advantages and disadvantages can multi-nationals bring to other countries?

Lucky Goldstar – lucky Wales?

In July 1996 the LG Group, a South Korean multi-national company, announced that it would invest £1.7 billion in an electronics complex close to Newport in South Wales. At the time it was the largest single inward investment to an EU region. Other **Development Agencies** in the UK had tried to attract LG but the company was convinced by the *Welsh Development Agency* that its aid package was best. The project, involving both LG Electronics and LG Semicon, was planned to create over 6 000 jobs directly.

Why Britain is the preferred destination

Britain is far and away the preferred destination in Europe for South Korean trans-national companies as they shift their location into the EU. Over 100 Korean manufacturers have settled in the UK with another thirteen to follow from March 1996. Why is this?

By settling in the EU, companies can avoid trade barriers that restrict export directly into Europe from South Korea.

- British wages are among the lowest in the EU whereas wages in South Korea are higher.
- Labour unrest in South Korea is a problem but in Britain strikes are rare.
- Britain offers a peaceful base compared with South Korea, which is worried about future nuclear action from North Korea.
- The English language is taught in all Korean schools; few study French or German.

What made LG choose Wales rather than another British region was because of the terms on offer. The Welsh Office and the Welsh Development Agency (WDA) offered a grant worth £200 million, or £30 000 for each of the 6 100 jobs that would be created. This was by far the most generous offer from any UK region.

Adapted from The Times, 11 July 1996

Why Wales? **A**

B LG – site and situation (1:50000)

Key

☐ LG factory site

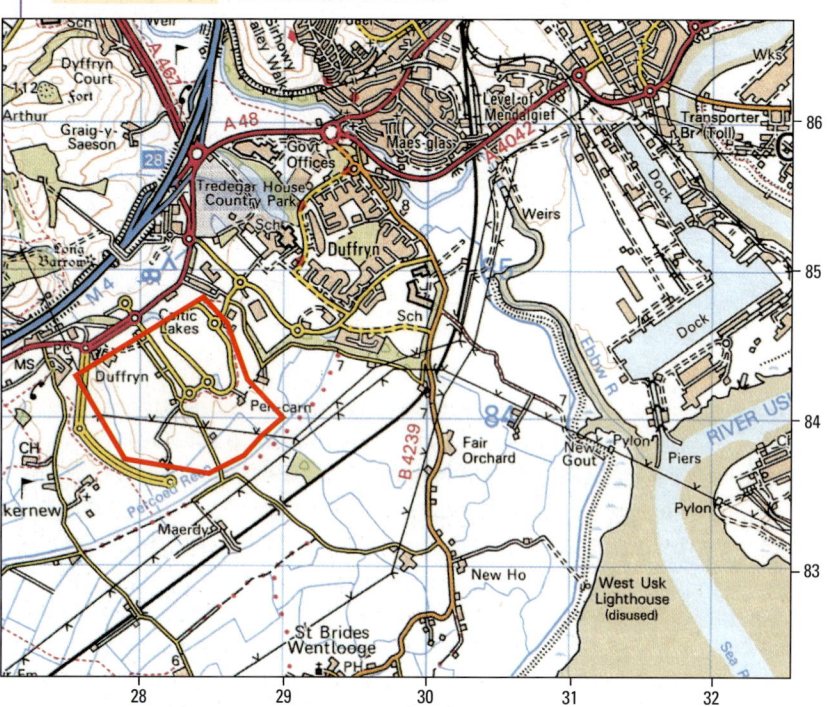

© Crown Copyright reserved

1 Study **Source A**.

a How many South Korean manufacturers were located in Britain by March 1996?

b List reasons for locating in Britain.

c Explain why LG decided to locate in South Wales.

2 Using evidence from **Sources B** and **C**:

a State from which direction the photo was taken.

b Draw an annotated sketch map to show the factory site. Refer to:
  - size
  - appearance
  - relief of the land
  - environmental impact.

c Suggest the attractions of this location for:
  - bringing in materials
  - distributing products
  - attracting workers.
  Give reasons for your answers.

d Suggest advantages and disadvantages for the local community of LG locating here. Refer to social, economic and environmental impacts.

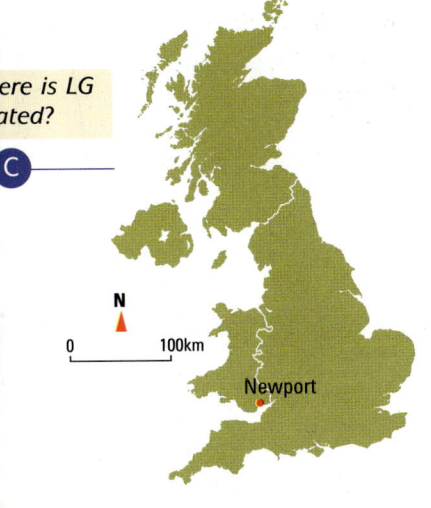

ere is LG
ated?

C

The multiplier effect

When a new factory opens, it creates job opportunities. This *direct employment* is in building the factory and in the factory itself. The factory will need to obtain materials from elsewhere and use services such as new roads or banks. Creating this extra *indirect employment* is known as **positive multiplier effect**.

Many multi-nationals, such as LG, have their headquarters outside the UK. If a company decides to close a factory in the UK, a **negative multiplier effect** can occur. Jobs are lost not only in the factory but also in other companies providing goods and services. As unemployed people spend less, many community shops and services also suffer. As the WDA has found out since 1998, circumstances in South Korea can cause the benefits of a major investment to be delayed!

A positive multiplier effect...

D

'The building of the factories has already provided jobs in construction. Most seeking jobs at LG will live within a reasonable travel-to-work radius of Newport but companies elsewhere can also benefit from LG. The two factories, employing over 6 000 people, will need materials from production-line robotics to toilet paper, and services from banking to window cleaning. We estimate there will be around 15 000 extra supplier and component jobs. Already 40 potential suppliers – 26 of them in Wales – have been visited by LG personnel.'

Mike Shukman – Welsh Development agency
Senior Executive responsible for LG

Global Crisis – local tragedy

No economy can continue to grow at the rate of Japan and South Korea. Eventually demand is satisfied and slows down. This causes an **economic recession**. As companies cannot sell their goods they produce less and make workers redundant until demand brings an **economic recovery**. Relying on multi-nationals is fine in boom years but they can pull out or downsize when economies go bust. In 1998 a financial crisis affected South Korea and other Asian economies…

APRIL 1998 – LG REVIEWS £1.7 BILLION INVESTMENT IN WALES

Although it is employing 2 500 workers at its LG Electronics factory near Newport, the LG company has decided not to open its LG Semicon plant due to the financial crisis in South Korea. The empty building has been sold to Hyundai, another South Korean multi-national. When the new owners have developed a new microchip it intends to open the factory. However the financial situation must be stable first…

3 Study **Source D**.
a What direct jobs were created or were expected to be created by the LG investment?
b How many indirect jobs were expected to be created elsewhere?
c Which suppliers are listed as examples? Add others from your own ideas.
d Explain the positive multiplier effect.

4 Study **Source E**.
a What is an economic recession?
b How has this affected LG's plans in South Wales?
c Suggest some negative multiplier effects of these revised plans.
d What hope is there for future investment in South Wales?

5 Study **Source F**. 'Relying on multi-national companies may bring advantages and disadvantages to the UK.' To what extent do you agree with this statement? Use evidence from pages 44-47.

F

E

...and recent negative multiplier effects!

MCDONALD'S PLANS MORE FAST-FOOD OUTLETS IN THE UK
December 2000

US giant Wal-Mart takes over ASDA and promises more stores and jobs
October 2000

BMW set to close Rover's Longbridge factory after six years – 6000 jobs to go
March 2000

Motorola to close Bathgate factory with loss of over 3000 jobs in Scotland
April 2001

3.6 Singapore – two routes for economic progress

Singapore – crossroads to Asia

Once a British colony, Singapore has been an independent **city state** since 1965. It has no natural resources although, in the last 40 years, it has become one of the most advanced manufacturing nations in South-East Asia.

Whereas Azerbaijan's route to economic development is based on primary industry, Singapore's economy is developing through secondary and tertiary industry.

A

Singapore – a brief history

In 1819 Sir Stamford Raffles wanted a base in South-East Asia for the British East India Company to trade from. After looking at maps he chose the island of Singapore, which consisted of mangrove swamps and a decrepit harbour. It was almost uninhabited: only 120 Malays and 20 Chinese lived there farming and fishing.

He bought this cheaply for the British after persuading the local sultans that they would benefit from trade as a British Colony. Singapore became an important base, an **entrêpot**, for the British to trade with the Far East and Hong Kong, another British colony.

Through Singapore came resources such as rubber and minerals from South-East Asia bound for Europe. Manufactured goods went in the reverse direction to South-East Asia. As the port developed it attracted international migrants for work. By 1911 Singapore had a population of 250 000 of 48 races speaking 54 languages.

Historical view of Singapore port

B

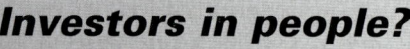

1942: Japanese invade and take over Singapore; a key defence location for the USA and UK.

1869: The Suez Canal was opened. This linked Europe and the Mediterranean Sea to the Red Sea and the Far East.

1946: British rule re-established. Chinese and Malayan communities fight for independence.

1956: Self-government for Singapore.

1963: Singapore becomes part of the Federation of Malaysia.

1965: Singapore becomes fully independent. Although lacking natural resources, Singapore becomes a wealthy city state in less than a generation.

C

Investors in people?

We don't want all this ... but the American tourists like it ... but for Singaporeans, we will go to sleep early. We will wake up early. Tomorrow we work hard ... Let the other fellow have a good time.

Prime Minister Lee Kuan Yew, 1965

To develop our economy we had to rely entirely on educating our people to a high standard and providing an attractive public image. We produce a workforce dedicated to making Singapore the best; unemployment is not allowed. We have had no strikes since 1965. The Singapore people share many qualities – a love of family, a penchant for hard work, and a pride in their origins. However, to stay ahead people must work even harder and be smarter if we are to become the first MEDC in tropical regions.

Prime Minister
Goh Chok Tong, 1997

1 Study **Source A**.
   a Suggest why Raffles chose Singapore as a base.
   b What primary industries were taking place?
   c What is an 'entrêpot'? Why did Singapore become an entrêpot?

2 Study **Source B**.
   a Use an atlas to help describe the location of Singapore.
   b Locate the Suez Canal. Suggest why 1869 was an important year for developing trade between Europe and the Far East.

3 Study **Source C**.
   a What qualities do both Prime Ministers say the people of Singapore have?
   b How much do you think these qualities have helped the country make rapid economic progress since 1965?

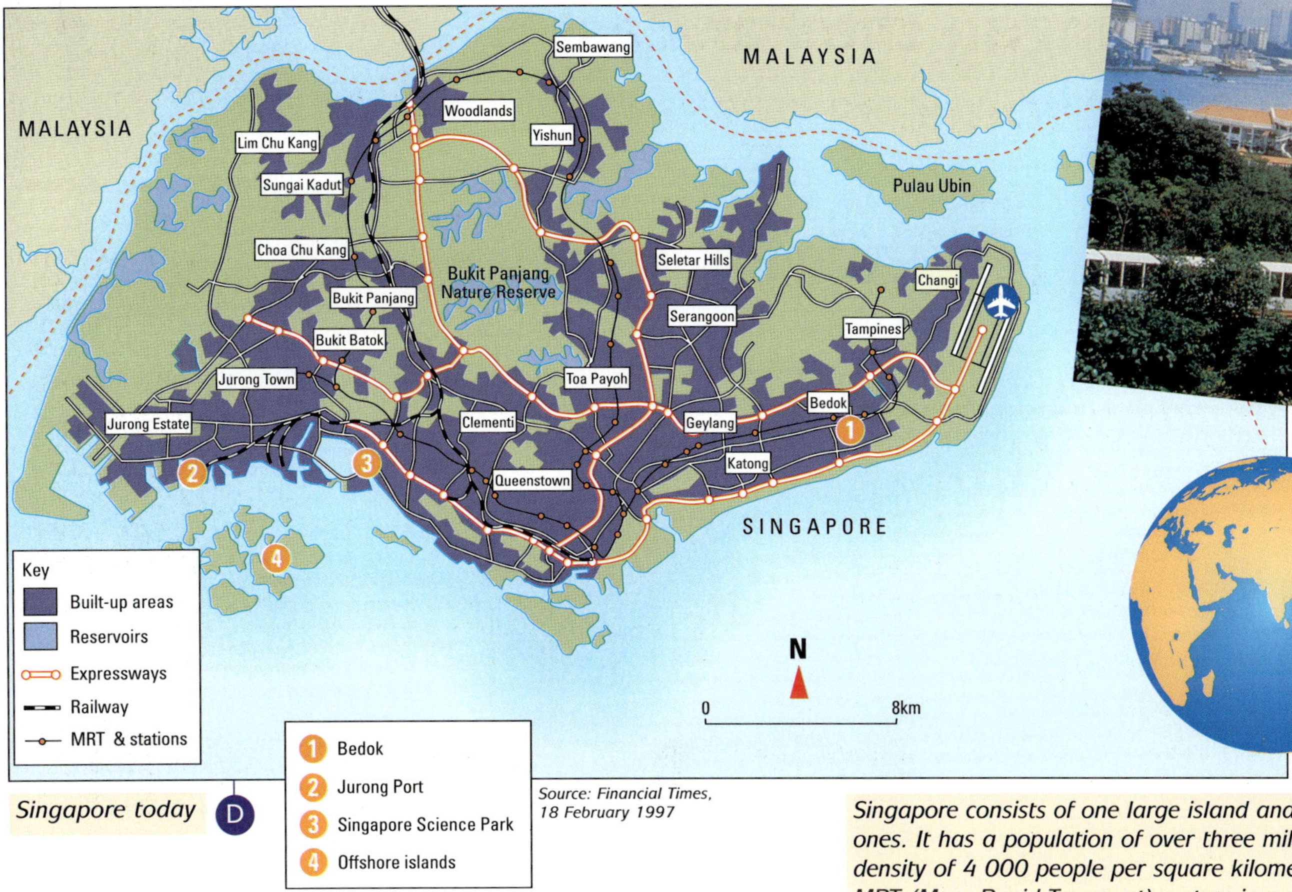

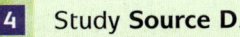

Key

- Built-up areas
- Reservoirs
- Expressways
- Railway
- MRT & stations

1 Bedok
2 Jurong Port
3 Singapore Science Park
4 Offshore islands

N
0   8km

MALAYSIA

Sembawang
Woodlands
Lim Chu Kang
Yishun
Sungai Kadut
Choa Chu Kang
Bukit Panjang Nature Reserve
Bukit Panjang
Bukit Batok
Seletar Hills
Changi
Serangoon
Jurong Town
Toa Payoh
Tampines
Jurong Estate
Clementi
Geylang
Bedok
Queenstown
Katong
SINGAPORE
MALAYSIA
Pulau Ubin

Singapore today (D)

Source: Financial Times, 18 February 1997

Singapore consists of one large island and many small ones. It has a population of over three million with a density of 4 000 people per square kilometre. The MRT (Mass Rapid Transport) system is a passenger train service that covers most parts of the city.

A variety of industrial centres (E)

1 Purpose-built industrial estates such as Bedok

These have been constructed close to new housing areas for labour supply and the expressways for delivery of components and finished products. The light industry concentrates on electrical goods and computers for export.

2 Jurong Port

Here is the largest concentration of industry. The port facilities exist for the import of raw materials. Here heavy industry concentrates on steelworks, shipbuilding and petrochemicals. These need large areas of flat land which has been drained from marshland or reclaimed from the sea. This is the busiest port in the world; a ship passes through every six minutes and there are usually 700 in port.

3 Singapore Science Park

Found in the south, close to the University and close to the major expressway. Firms producing computers and hi tech equipment are located here. They provide the university with funds; in return they benefit from research and development (R & D) ideas.

4 Offshore islands to the south

Here are the main oil refining centres. Crude oil is delivered from Brunei and refined here into a range of fuels and oil-based products. Pipelines connect to the mainland supplying the petro-chemical industries at Jurong with fuel.

4 Study **Source D**.
- a Estimate the area of Singapore.
- b Describe the distribution of:
  - built-up areas
  - transport links.
- c What evidence is there that:
  - demand for water is high
  - space is limited?

5 Study **Source E**.
- a Describe the distribution of the purpose-built industrial estates.
- b How is the distribution of heavy industry different? Why?
- c What does the abbreviation 'R & D' mean?
- d Suggest why some firms locate close to universities.

6 Imagine you work for the *Singapore Economic Development Board*. You have been asked to produce an annotated map of Singapore that shows:
- the infrastructure available for new industries
- the variety of industrial centres.
- a Produce your map.
- b Justify what you have chosen to illustrate.

3.7 Investing in the Far East

Forty years of change...with more to come

A

% people employed in	1957	1977	1997
Primary industry	9	3	1
Secondary industry	17	25	35
Tertiary industry	74	72	64

Hewlett Packard (computers) is one example of a multi-national company manufacturing products in Singapore

Multi-national finance companies provide inward investment

A great deal of investment is taking place in South-East Asia and the Far East. Because of this many banks, insurance companies, fund managers and financial institutions are locating headquarters close to these growing economies. In 1997 CGU (now CGU-Norwich Union) decided to locate a new regional headquarters in Singapore. From here it could manage its Asia–Pacific fund more effectively, being closer to the places it was investing in.

C

CGU-Norwich Union has its regional headquarters in Singapore

Despite a financial crisis in the Far East since 1998, Prime Minister Goh Chok Tong has a clear message about the future of Singapore. In an interview he was asked the following question.

Question: *'Throughout the crisis, Singapore has focused on its long-term objectives such as taking a lead in the IT area. Why is this so important to Singapore?'*

Answer: *'We see this as the future growth area. Electronic commerce, ability to write software programs, linking up with other e-commerce centres in the world – it is going to be a growth area. Just look at the IT stocks, Internet stocks, the value which they have created for those with the websites and the ideas. We, therefore, want to move into this growth area. It will also enable us to increase the productivity for banking, for business, for your office work. We want to widen the distance between ourselves and others.'*

Source: Financial Times, 31 March 1999

We operate a network of international offices in the USA, Japan and SE Asia. We aim to generate interest in inward investment in Singapore and to service existing investors. We help businesses obtain:

- *cheap land*
- *factories and offices designed and built to investor requirements*
- *loans at low rates of interest*
- *cheap, hard-working labour*
- *local suppliers.*

It also provides the ideal location for American and European businesses who want a half-way base to the markets of SE Asia.

Singapore Economic Development Board

B

What the SEDB does ...

GRAVE CONCERN IN SINGAPORE

With Singapore running out of graveyard space, cremation is the only way of prolonging the lifespan of the island's last cemetery. It will be full in 15 years. All of Singapore's private cemeteries have already closed.

A grave situation D

Source: Adapted from The Times

Service industries have changed

Rapid economic growth has created enormous wealth for Singapore. The government has used this to develop a better infrastructure and increase job opportunities in new service industries such as education, banking and financial services. Most of the new services industries have their main headquarters in MEDCs but need a regional base to access growing markets in the Far East such as China. However Singapore is determined to be a world leader in its own right in the ICT industry; it is in this sector that most of the country's investment is taking place.

1 a Plot the information from **Source A** on a triangular graph.
  b Describe how Singapore's employment structure changed between 1957 and 1997.
  c On your graph, predict where the employment structure will be in 2017.

2 Study **Source B**.
  a How does the SEDB raise awareness of opportunities in Singapore?
  b What incentives can it offer new businesses?

3 Study **Source C**.
  a Explain why Commercial Union located in Singapore in 1997.
  b Suggest other overseas companies that could use the ICT services being developed in Singapore.
  c Why does the Prime Minister want Singapore to take a global lead in developing an ICT industry?
  d Suggest a disadvantage in basing future development on the Internet and ICT growth.

4 Study **Sources C** and **D**.
  a Read **Source D**. How does it help explain the view in the photograph of Singapore?
  b What problem exists for future development in Singapore? Suggest **two** other solutions to create more space.

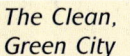

The Clean, Green City **E**

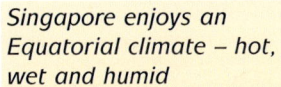

NEW ASIA

Singapore

So easy to enjoy, so hard to forget.

New Asia Heartlands of Singapore

Daily (Except Sunday & Public Holidays)

Pick-up time	: 14:00 hrs
Tour starts	: 14:30 hrs
Duration	: 3½ hrs

Tour Price:
Adult : S$28.00
Child : S$14.00

From rustic charm to futuristic city. Experience a slice of life in a typical Malay community in the 50s and 60s, then drive through the predominantly Peranakan and Eurasian heartlands of Singapore and see the eclectic architecture, combining European Corinthian columns and brightly-coloured Chinese decorative motifs. The view gives in more quiet, idyllic surroundings as we head further towards the eastern tip of the island, Changi, where we revel in the scene of a beachside village setting, and pause to reflect on our history and the events that helped shape our present day Singapore with a stop at the Changi prison Chapel and Museum.

We then proceed to Tampines New Town for a glimpse of a typical satellite town. Wired for the future, we enjoy the best of modern technology, but still hold dear centuries-old traditions and cultural practices, as seen in the worship of ancestors at a typical Taoist Temple.

THE BEST 2 DAILY COACH TOURS

Booking office:

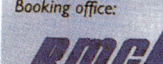

RMG TOURS PTE LTD
109C Amoy Street Singapore 069929
Tel: 2201661 (5 Lines) Tlx: Tours RS 23831 Fax: 3246530
E-mail: rmgtours@signet.com.sg
GST Reg No: M2-0020463-8

The annual Courtesy Campaign began in 1979. It helps make Singapore a warm, friendly place for residents and visitors.

Singapore

**No litter
No graffiti
No spitting
No smoking in public places
No chewing gum**

F Singapore enjoys an Equatorial climate – hot, wet and humid

	J	F	M	A	M	J	J	A	S	O	N	D
Temperature (°C)	27	28	28	29	28	28	28	27	27	27	27	27
Precipitation (mm)	250	170	192	190	175	172	170	193	180	205	250	255
Average sunshine hours	5	7	6	6	6	6	6	6	5	5	5	4

A Singapore stop-over

The *Singapore Tourist Promotion Board* (STPB) was established in 1964. Since independence, Singapore's tourist industry has enjoyed rapid growth. With cheaper long-haul air flights, the Far East has become a fashionable and accessible region to visit. For Europeans, Singapore provides the perfect stopping-off place as a break in a long journey to South-East Asia and Australia. It now attracts tourists in its own right, increasing job opportunities in the tertiary industry. Today more people visit Singapore than live there!

5 Study **Sources E** and **F**.
a List the attractions you might see on one of the RMG tours of the island.
b Why do you think Singapore is known as the 'clean, green city'?
c Suggest **one** advantage and **one** disadvantage of Singapore's climate for tourists.
d List the different job opportunities that tourists are likely to bring to the people of Singapore.

6 Imagine you work for a bank, insurance or ICT company in the UK. The company is going to open up a branch in Singapore. You have been asked to work there on a two-year contract.
a What would your initial reaction be to the offer? Explain your view.
b Make a list of questions you would want to ask about living and working in Singapore before you decide on the offer.

3 At a junction near you...

To the north and west (M6) and east (A14)

M1 Motorway

To Europe via Willesdon and the Channel Tunnel

To London and the South

To Birmingham and the North-West

West-coast line

To Europe via Willesdon and the Channel Tunnel

DIRFT from the air

(A) — circle label

The location of DIRFT (B)

OS Rugby and Daventry 1:25 000

Crick Covert

Covert Lodge

The Cedars

(C) Who's there now...who's coming? (April 2001)

Photo ref.	Company	Business	Status
1 & 8	Eddie Stobart	Lorry distribution	Built and expanding
2	The Malcolm Group	Lorry distribution	Built and expanding
3	Ingram Micro	Lorry distribution	Built
4	Tibbett & Britten	Own the railport	Built and expanding
5	Tesco	Lorry distribution	Under construction
6	Holiday Inn	Hotel/conferences	Built
7	Knights of Old	Lorry distribution	Site acquired

(D) Why here? HEADS

Access to J18 of the M1 motorway...
Central location in the UK...
Fairly flat land...
No competition from other land uses...
Close to large towns and cities...
Land is not built on...
Nobody lives there...
Direct rail line for freight to Europe from West and Midlands
Large site...

(E) Why here? TAILS

...so time saved accessing motorway network
...so easy to travel north, south, east or west
...so low costs in levelling surface for building
...so land relatively cheap
...so labour easy to access
...so no delay in removing existing buildings
...so no local opposition to the plans
...so rapid link to and from the EU and eastern European markets
...so room for large warehouses and expansion

A central location for a logistics park

All companies that produce goods require an efficient **infrastructure** to distribute them quickly. How this is done using different transport links is known as **logistics**. The *Daventry International Rail Freight Terminal* (DIRFT) is a logistics park under construction near Junction 18 of the M1 motorway. Large companies with outlets all over the UK and links with Europe are setting up warehouses at DIRFT for product distribution by road and rail. This is an example of a tertiary industrial location as most companies locating here are providing a transport service for other companies.

1 Study **Sources A** and **B**.
a Draw a sketch map to show:
 • the M1 motorway, J18 and the main roads
 • the DIRFT site and its buildings
 • the railway line.
b On the map, name the company buildings and their status (numbered 1-8 on **Source C**).

2 Study **Sources D** and **E**.
a Match the HEADS with the TAILS.
b Label and annotate your sketch map to show why the DIRFT site has been created here.

3 Carry out a similar research study into building developments near to a motorway or major road junction in your own area.

4

Economic activity and the environment

KEY IDEAS

Economic activity can seriously damage the physical environment.

Plains have been put forward to build the world's highest hotel close to one of mount Everest's base camps.

4.1 Industrial rise and fall

Why do industries rise and decline?

What are the effects of traditional industries on the environment?

A timeline of developments in the steel-making process **B**

The location of the Ruhr **A**

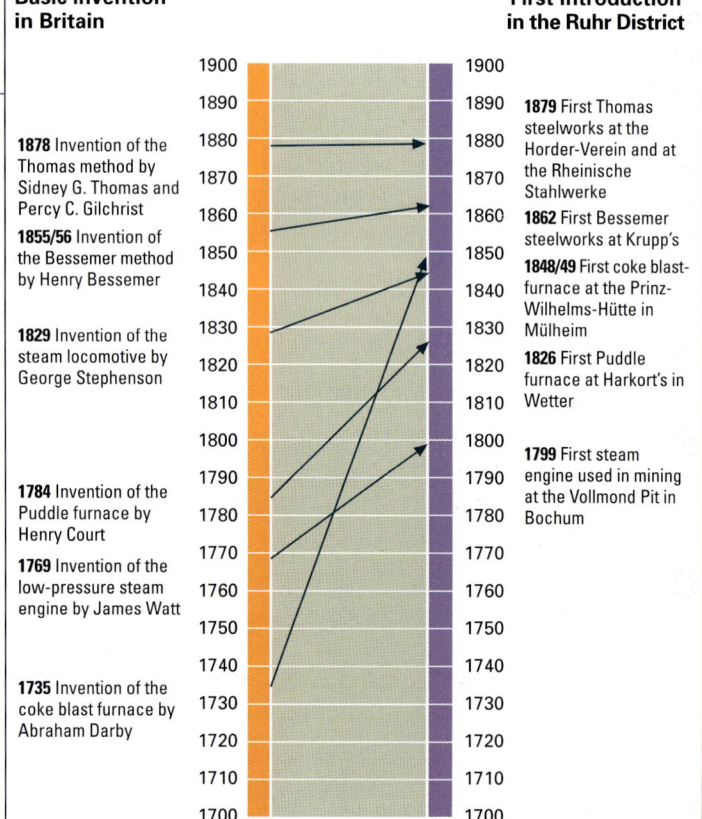

Basic invention in Britain		First introduction in the Ruhr District
	1900	1900
	1890	1890 **1879** First Thomas steelworks at the Horder-Verein and at the Rheinische Stahlwerke
1878 Invention of the Thomas method by Sidney G. Thomas and Percy C. Gilchrist	1880	1880
	1870	1870
1855/56 Invention of the Bessemer method by Henry Bessemer	1860	1860 **1862** First Bessemer steelworks at Krupp's
	1850	1850 **1848/49** First coke blast-furnace at the Prinz-Wilhelms-Hütte in Mülheim
	1840	1840
1829 Invention of the steam locomotive by George Stephenson	1830	1830 **1826** First Puddle furnace at Harkort's in Wetter
	1820	1820
	1810	1810
	1800	1800 **1799** First steam engine used in mining at the Vollmond Pit in Bochum
1784 Invention of the Puddle furnace by Henry Court	1790	1790
	1780	1780
1769 Invention of the low-pressure steam engine by James Watt	1770	1770
	1760	1760
	1750	1750
	1740	1740
1735 Invention of the coke blast furnace by Abraham Darby	1730	1730
	1720	1720
	1710	1710
	1700	1700

A slow start

During the first half of the nineteenth century, the United Kingdom was well into its 'Industrial Revolution'. At this time the Ruhr district of Germany was still mainly a rural community although some **smelting** of iron took place using charcoal. The Ruhr developed rapidly as an industrial area between 1840 and 1880. It did so by importing technology from the UK and copying and improving it. Industrial rise was rapid and coalmines, steelworks, railways and heavy industries were established based on local resources of coal and iron ore. This rapid expansion of primary and secondary activities continued in the twentieth century causing industrial damage and eventual dereliction.

The Ruhr district – an area of heavy industry **C**

1 Use **Source A** to help describe the location of the Ruhr district.

2 Study **Source B**.
   a How long did it take for the following inventions to reach the Ruhr:
      • the coke blast furnace
      • the Puddle furnace
      • the Thomas method?
   b Describe how the delay changed with time. Suggest why.

3 a Draw a sketch of **Source C**.
   b Label it to show features likely to cause damage to the environment.
   c Add annotations to explain the types of damage caused.

Environmental decline

During the Second World War (1939-1945), much of the Ruhr's heavy industry was destroyed by bombing. Although some rebuilding took place, there was less demand for the products of heavy industry in Europe. There was also increased competition from new producers in other parts of the world. Just like the UK coal and steel industry, the Ruhr region went into a rapid decline. Since the mid-1970s there has been little left apart from the legacy of severe scarring of the landscape that the industry has left behind.

4 Give **three** reasons why the Ruhr went into rapid decline.

5 a Describe what is happening in **Source D**.
b Outline the economic and environmental changes affecting the local and national government.

6 Look at **Source E**.
a Explain how both negative and positive multipliers have worked in the area.
b Suggest why the spiral could be called 'The rise, fall and rise again' of the Ruhr.
c What links exist between industrial development and the environment?
d Where in the spiral would you place **Source C**? Why?

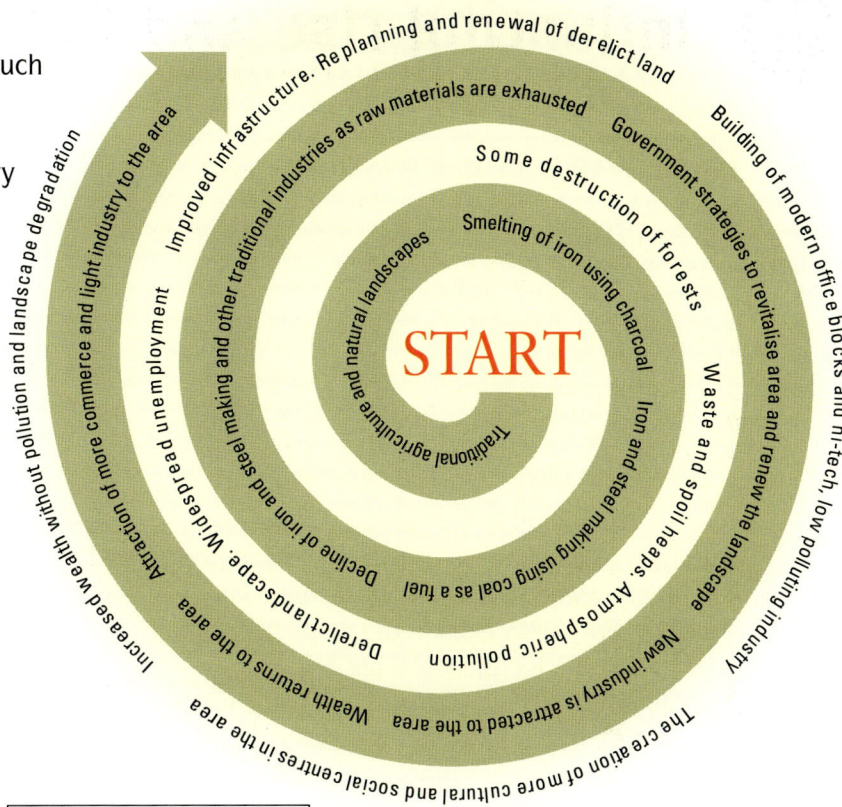

START

Traditional agriculture and natural landscapes
Smelting of iron using charcoal
Some destruction of forests
Iron and steel making using coal as a fuel
Government strategies to revitalise area and renew the landscape
Waste and spoil heaps. Atmospheric pollution
Building of modern office blocks and hi-tech, low polluting industry
New industry is attracted to the area
Replanning and renewal of derelict land
Decline of iron and steel making and other traditional industries as raw materials are exhausted
Derelict landscape. Widespread unemployment
Improved infrastructure.
Attraction of more commerce and light industry to the area
Increased wealth without pollution and landscape degradation
Wealth returns to the area
Decline of iron and steel making and other traditional industries
The creation of more cultural and social centres in the area

Key
Industrial activity
Effects of industrial activity

E *A spiral of development in the Ruhr*

D *The closure of one of the last remaining Ruhr steelworks*

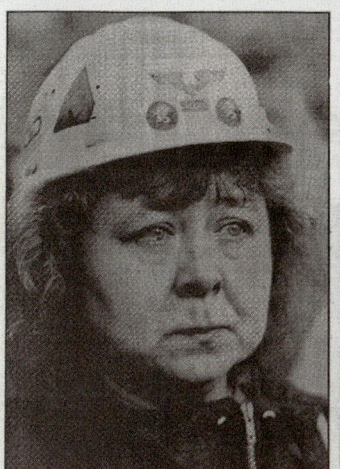

THE GUARDIAN
Saturday March 13 1993

EUROPEAN BUSINESS 39

Trouble at mill... A female steel worker (above) sheds tears at a demonstration against Krupp's proposal to close the Duisburg-Rheinhausen mill (right, with rolls of steel in foreground) at a cost of 2,000 jobs. The shutdown, due on March 31, has been postponed to permit an independent examination of the case for closure, amid allegations that the books were 'cooked' against the mill. There is, however, little hope that the company will make a U-turn.

4.2 Repairing the damage

Renewing the Emscher Region

'The Emscher Region has a lot to offer in the way of greenery when looked at from a bird's eye view. But anyone trying to find beauty spots on foot or by bicycle soon comes across features typical of the Ruhr district: industrial sites, sewers, roads and railway lines.'

IBA Emscher Park Gelsenkirchen, 1995

In order to change this situation, seventeen Emscher towns linked with the *Association of Ruhr District Local Authorities* to create the 'Emscher Park'. No extra money has been made available for the work but the programme they have devised receives money from a total of 36 State aid programmes. One-third of the other money needed to create the Park comes from private investors and the other two-thirds from State funds. The Emscher Park has five central themes aimed at meeting the needs of the region's people and environment to ensure a sustainable future.

1 The Emscher Landscape Park

Area: 500 square kilometres

Finance: Emscher-Lippe Ecology Programme

Timescale: 20–30 years

Detail: the creation of a main east to west green corridor with seven smaller north to south corridors. It includes everything from the redevelopment of large areas of derelict land to the planting of small areas of trees.

Gladbec

Bottrop

Oberhausen

Mülheim

Duisburg

River Rhine

2 Ecological regeneration of the Emscher river system

Scale: 550 kilometres of waste water courses

Finance: sewerage charges

Timescale: 20–30 years

Detail: redesigning water courses, the construction of new sewerage treatment plants and the ecological treatment of rainwater.

3 Working in the Park

Area: 500 hectares

Finance: regional and EU grants, private investment

Timescale: 5–7 years

Detail: work at over 20 different locations to create modern commerce, services and science parks. All are built on former industrial sites. These are accompanied by start-up centres for new businesses and technology centres designed to attract high-tech business.

4 Housing construction and integrated urban district development

Dwellings: 6 000

Finance: regional and national grants. Private investment

Timescale: 2–5 years

Detail: 26 individual projects re-using vacant sites to build about 3 000 new flats. Also the refurbishing of 3 000 existing flats. About three-quarters of the new housing will be public sector rented accommodation. Some, including those in the photograph, were planned by women with the needs of women in mind.

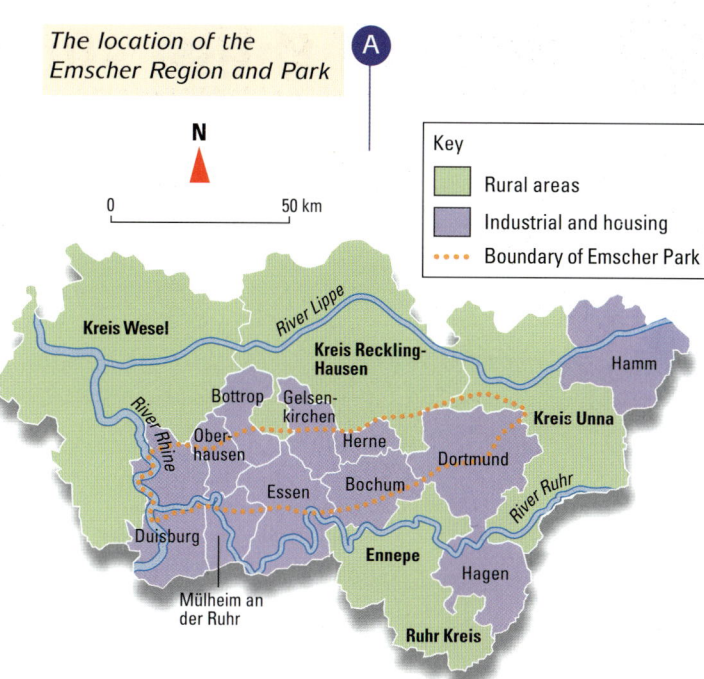

The location of the Emscher Region and Park **A**

Key

Rural areas

Industrial and housing

Boundary of Emscher Park

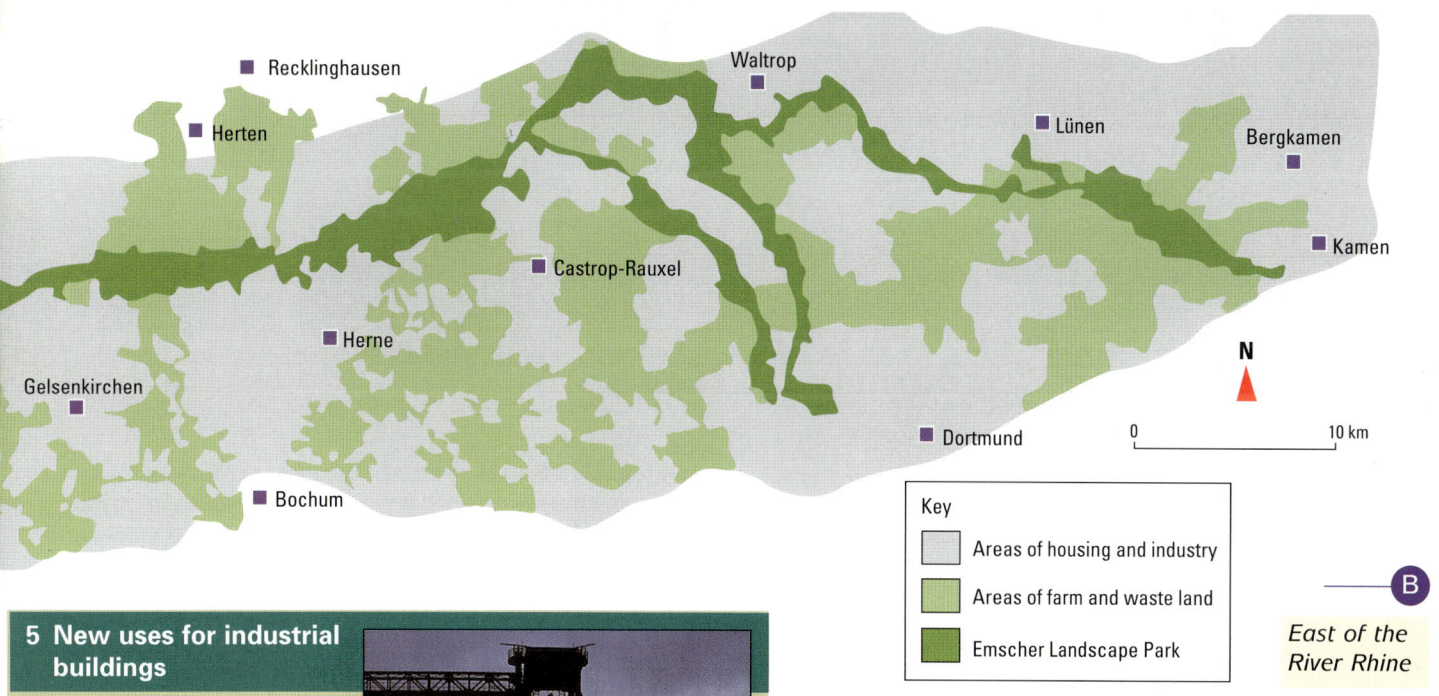

Key

Areas of housing and industry

Areas of farm and waste land

Emscher Landscape Park

East of the River Rhine **B**

5 New uses for industrial buildings

Projects: 27

Finance: national and EU funding, and private investment

Timescale: 2–5 years

Detail: keeping some of the relics of the industrial past in place and converting them to modern use. Among the examples are the use of the inside of a gasometer as an exhibition hall and pithead buildings as a centre for art and culture.

1 Study **Source A**. Describe the location of the Emscher Region within the Ruhr.

2 Use **Source B** to help you write a report on the development of the Emscher Region. Comment on each of the following:
- environmental improvements
- improvements in living conditions
- increased work opportunities.

3 To what extent do you feel it is possible to manage an area in a sustainable way so that it meets the needs of its people without damaging the environment?

4.3 Beyond these shores

A *Getting to the seaside – an early away day*

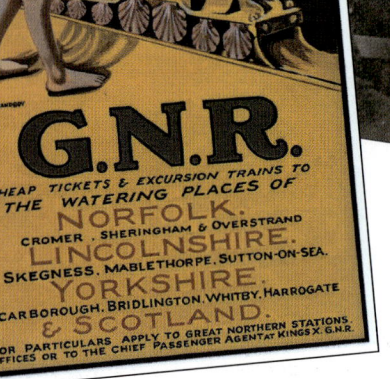

G.N.R.
CHEAP TICKETS & EXCURSION TRAINS TO
THE WATERING PLACES OF
NORFOLK.
CROMER, SHERINGHAM & OVERSTRAND
LINCOLNSHIRE.
SKEGNESS, MABLETHORPE, SUTTON-ON-SEA.
YORKSHIRE.
SCARBOROUGH, BRIDLINGTON, WHITBY, HARROGATE
& SCOTLAND.
FOR PARTICULARS APPLY TO GREAT NORTHERN STATIONS,
OFFICES OR TO THE CHIEF PASSENGER AGENT AT KINGS X, G.N.R.

Who goes abroad?

C

Percentage of adults taking a holiday (1998)		
	A holiday abroad	A holiday in Great Britain
Britain	38	31
Wales	34	36
Scotland	35	32
England	39	31
Standard Regions of England		
North	40	26
North-West	43	26
Yorkshire & Humberside	38	37
East Midlands	39	36
West Midlands	36	29
East Anglia	29	33
South East	43	29
South West	32	37

Source: Regional Trends 1999

Sir Freddie Laker was the first entrepreneur to offer cheap flights to European holiday destinations

B

LAKER TAKES DELIVERY OF HIS FIRST DC10

Freddie Laker, aviation entrepreneur and thorn in the side of the big established airlines, took delivery of his first DC10 today. It will go into service on the 'sunshine' routes, flying holidaymakers to the Mediterranean region.

12 November 1972

From Blackpool to Benidorm

Before the mid 1800s, only the very rich travelled far from their homes. This situation changed with the Industrial Revolution as more people left farming to work in factories and the rail network expanded. This gave access to the seaside and resorts began to grow as factory owners organised day trips for workers. Later, as workers were given paid holidays and road and rail networks spread further, many workers used their own cars to spend a week or two at a seaside resort. The traditional British seaside holiday had begun.

In the 1950s and early 1960s, most UK holidaymakers visited UK resorts or went by road and ferry to European destinations. In the late 1960s, cheap air flights began to the Mediterranean resorts especially those in Spain. Demand was created for package holidays and many Spanish fishing villages became tourist resorts almost overnight as hotels were quickly built. By this time people had longer holidays and greater disposable income. They had the money, time and transport to go abroad for their holidays. Spain and its islands remain the first choice summer holiday destination for Britons.

1 Study **Source A**.
a What is the message of the postcard?
b Imagine you are a person in the photo. It is your first seaside trip and you are sending a postcard to a friend. What would you write?

2 Study **Source B** and the text.
a Give **three** reasons why people were able to take holidays outside the UK.
b Suggest how the changed holiday patterns may have affected:
  • the owner of a Blackpool fish & chips shop
  • householders living near a British airport
  • children living in a Spanish fishing village
  • the environment of the Spanish coast.

3 Study **Source C**.
a Draw a graph to show the holiday pattern for the region where you live.
b How does your region compare with the other UK regions in terms of:
  • holidays abroad
  • holidays in the UK?
c Suggest reasons for your findings.

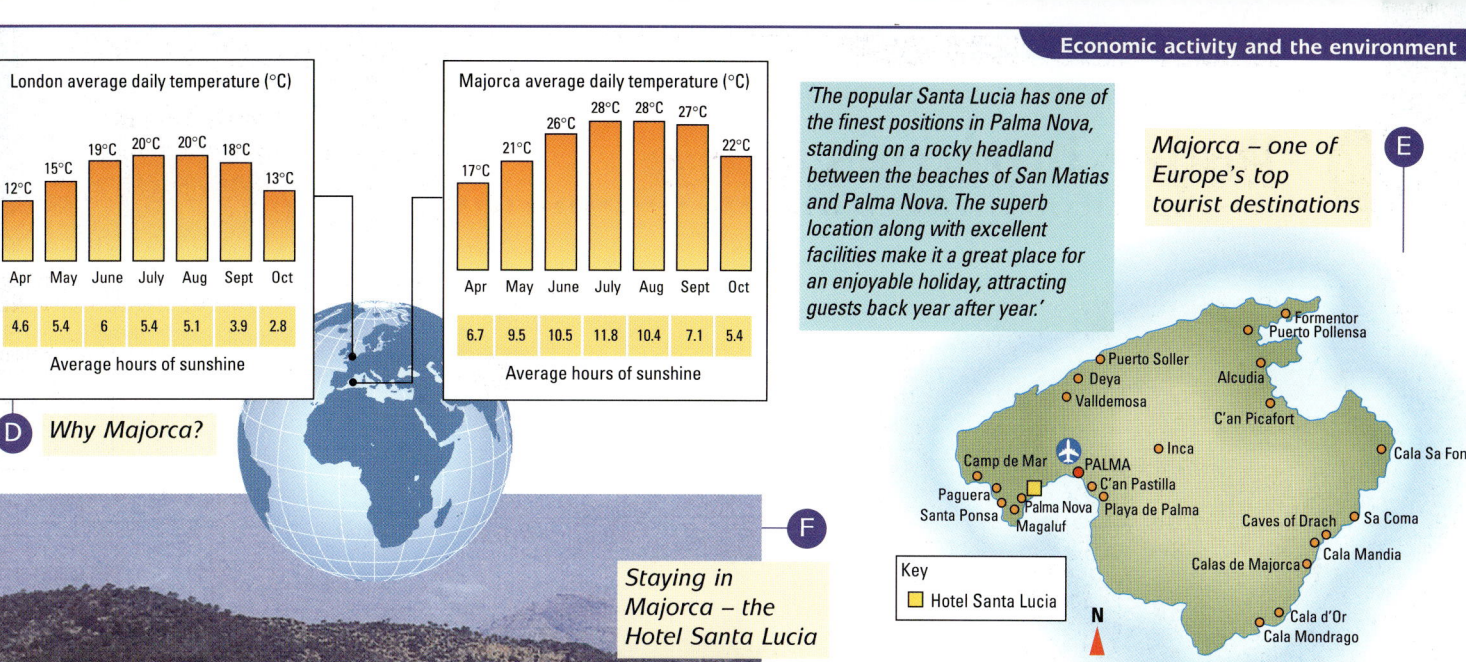

London average daily temperature (°C)

Apr	May	June	July	Aug	Sept	Oct
12°C	15°C	19°C	20°C	20°C	18°C	13°C

Average hours of sunshine

| 4.6 | 5.4 | 6 | 5.4 | 5.1 | 3.9 | 2.8 |

Majorca average daily temperature (°C)

Apr	May	June	July	Aug	Sept	Oct
17°C	21°C	26°C	28°C	28°C	27°C	22°C

Average hours of sunshine

| 6.7 | 9.5 | 10.5 | 11.8 | 10.4 | 7.1 | 5.4 |

D *Why Majorca?*

'The popular Santa Lucia has one of the finest positions in Palma Nova, standing on a rocky headland between the beaches of San Matias and Palma Nova. The superb location along with excellent facilities make it a great place for an enjoyable holiday, attracting guests back year after year.'

E *Majorca – one of Europe's top tourist destinations*

Formentor
Puerto Pollensa
Puerto Soller
Deya
Valldemosa
Alcudia
C'an Picafort
Inca
Cala Sa Font
Camp de Mar
PALMA
C'an Pastilla
Paguera
Santa Ponsa
Palma Nova
Playa de Palma
Magaluf
Caves of Drach
Sa Coma
Calas de Majorca
Cala Mandia
Cala d'Or
Cala Mondrago

Key
□ Hotel Santa Lucia

N

0   10   20km

F *Staying in Majorca – the Hotel Santa Lucia*

Location of Hotel Santa Lucia
- Central location right on the beach, with access to a new promenade which skirts the seaward side of the hotel.
- A few steps from the terrace lead to the sandy beach.
- The resort centre is 400m away and there is a wealth of coffee shops, bars and restaurants right on the doorstep.

G *Some environmental issues*

Tourists face tax

Madrid, Barcelona and several resorts popular with Britons on the north-east coast of Spain are considering a tourist tax of one euro (62p) for each night that a guest spends in a hotel or a holiday flat. The money would be spent on environmental improvements.

Source: The Times, 27 April 2001

'We had to rethink the tourist strategy for Majorca when the water supply ran out in 1994. So much fresh water was being used that its supply was unsustainable. The local water turned salty and the residents and visitors had to rely on shipments of freshwater from Barcelona. To prevent this happening again we opened a desalination plant in 1998 which provides sustainable supplies of water to meet demand. We also introduced the Law of Golf which applies to the whole island. Only waste water can be used on the courses so that does not use up any fresh water.

We were also concerned about improving the appearance of the environment for future generations. Calvia is a district of 30 000 people on the island which attracts 1.2 million visitors. Here many high-rise hotels were built hastily in Magaluf and Palm Nova in the 1960s/1970s causing visual ugliness. Now they are being upgraded, or torn down to be replaced by green spaces. Zoning laws affect further development. Calvia was commended in the European Sustainable City Awards.'
Spokesperson for the Majorca Tourist Authority

4 Study **Source D**.
a Describe the temperature pattern for Majorca between April and October.
b How does this compare with London?
c Compare the sunshine hours in London and Majorca.
d Suggest reasons for the differences you have described.

5 Study **Sources E** and **F**.
a Describe the location of the Hotel Santa Lucia with regard to Palma airport.
b Write your own version of the hotel's location. Would this attract you to stay here?

6 a On an outline copy of the photo in **Source F** label:
   - features of the natural environment
   - features of the built environment.
b Annotate your sketch to show how the tourist industry and the activities available for tourists affect the environment in and around this hotel.

7 Study **Source G**.
a In what ways were tourist activities causing problems by 1994?
b What have the authorities done to make tourism more sustainable on Majorca?
c What is your view of the proposed 'tourist tax'?

4.4 Wider horizons

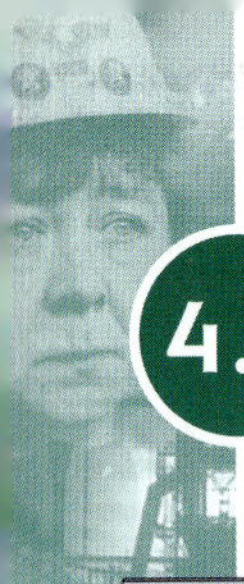

What attracts tourists to destinations beyond Europe?

What conflicts may tourists cause for local people and the environment?

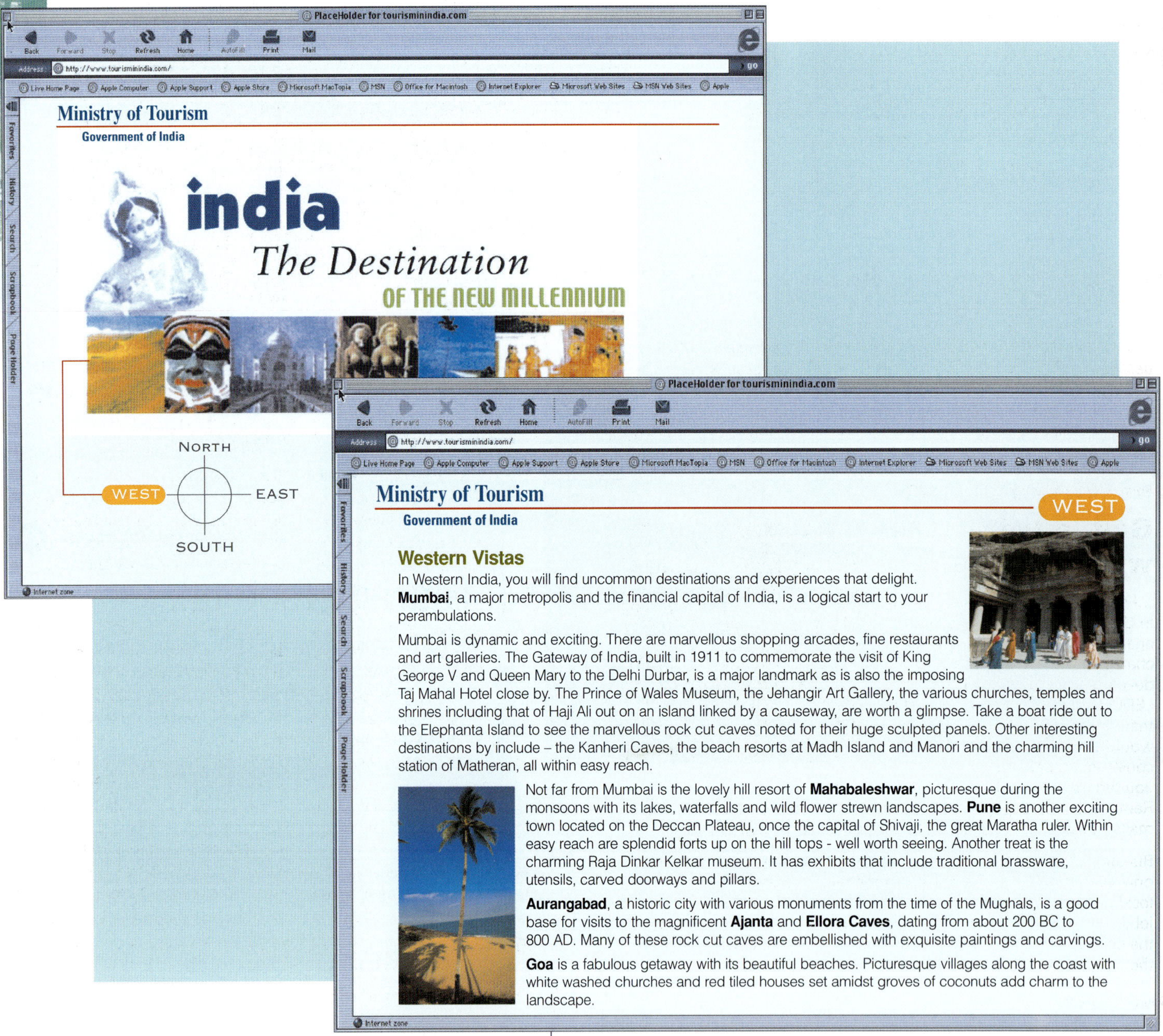
PlaceHolder for tourisminindia.com
Back
Forward
Stop
Refresh
Home
AutoFill
Print
Mail
Address
http://www.tourisminindia.com/
go
Live Home Page
Apple Computer
Apple Support
Apple Store
Microsoft MacTopia
MSN
Office for Macintosh
Internet Explorer
Microsoft Web Sites
MSN Web Sites
Apple
Favorites
History
Search
Scrapbook
Page Holder
Ministry of Tourism
Government of India
india
The Destination
OF THE NEW MILLENNIUM
NORTH
WEST
EAST
SOUTH
Internet zone
PlaceHolder for tourisminindia.com
Ministry of Tourism
Government of India
WEST
Western Vistas
In Western India, you will find uncommon destinations and experiences that delight. Mumbai, a major metropolis and the financial capital of India, is a logical start to your perambulations.
Mumbai is dynamic and exciting. There are marvellous shopping arcades, fine restaurants and art galleries. The Gateway of India, built in 1911 to commemorate the visit of King George V and Queen Mary to the Delhi Durbar, is a major landmark as is also the imposing Taj Mahal Hotel close by. The Prince of Wales Museum, the Jehangir Art Gallery, the various churches, temples and shrines including that of Haji Ali out on an island linked by a causeway, are worth a glimpse. Take a boat ride out to the Elephanta Island to see the marvellous rock cut caves noted for their huge sculpted panels. Other interesting destinations by include – the Kanheri Caves, the beach resorts at Madh Island and Manori and the charming hill station of Matheran, all within easy reach.
Not far from Mumbai is the lovely hill resort of Mahabaleshwar, picturesque during the monsoons with its lakes, waterfalls and wild flower strewn landscapes. Pune is another exciting town located on the Deccan Plateau, once the capital of Shivaji, the great Maratha ruler. Within easy reach are splendid forts up on the hill tops - well worth seeing. Another treat is the charming Raja Dinkar Kelkar museum. It has exhibits that include traditional brassware, utensils, carved doorways and pillars.
Aurangabad, a historic city with various monuments from the time of the Mughals, is a good base for visits to the magnificent Ajanta and Ellora Caves, dating from about 200 BC to 800 AD. Many of these rock cut caves are embellished with exquisite paintings and carvings.
Goa is a fabulous getaway with its beautiful beaches. Picturesque villages along the coast with white washed churches and red tiled houses set amidst groves of coconuts add charm to the landscape.
Internet zone

www.tourisminindia.com/indiathedestination.htm **A**

Tourism aids development...

Travel and tourism is one of the world's fastest growing industries. Long-haul tourism, mainly from Europe, Japan and North America, has expanded rapidly. The World Tourism Organisation (WTO) estimates that tourism creates 11 per cent of the world's GDP. Many LEDCs are exploiting their natural and cultural resources to attract the tourists who bring such welcome foreign income with them.

1 a Use **Source A** to help you complete a table like the one below.

Tourist features of India			
Beach	Other natural features	History	Other cultural features
Beach resort at Madh Island, Mumbai			

b Which places advertised on the web page would you most like to visit Why?

...but sometimes at a price!

There are few places in the world where tourism has not had an effect on both the environment and the lives of local people. While LEDCs need tourism to create jobs and generate income, it often also creates social, environmental and economic issues. Today there is concern about the negative impacts of global tourism and ways of ensuring that it is sustainable are being investigated.

Could you look a bit more ... authentic?

Photo by John McConnico

B

Social and cultural issues – 'ethical photography' in Rajasthan, India

Tourists taking photographs of children selling dung at Pushkar Camel Fair

Economic issues – employment in Mumbai and Goa **C**

'...near Mumbai there are historic caves which are a popular day-trip destination. Climbing several hundreds steps you are assaulted by trinket sellers, café owners, monkeys and most bizarrely, village women with empty metal pots on their heads. They insist you take a picture then ask for money. Although they use plastic buckets in their day-to-day lives they use metal ones deliberately dented to give an authentic look for tourists.'

Source: The Observer, 25 March 2001

Golf in India – the wrong course?

...For more than five years people in Goa and Karnataka have been against more golf courses. Those in charge of the game are keen to develop more tournaments in LEDCs which also want the prestige that global coverage brings. This would benefit hotel entrepreneurs, construction industries, golf equipment manufacturers and airline industries. Hotel groups like Ramada see the real profits in developing luxury hotels, shopping malls, retirement villages and tennis courts in the golf complex.

Building a golf course creates about 300 jobs during construction and only 40 in running it. The hi-tech equipment creates few jobs for the local people who would mainly carry out low-skill and low-income jobs such as waiters, waitresses, shop clerks and labourers. Most of the economic wealth generated by golf developments will flow out of the country into overseas investors and multi-national companies.

Source: Tourism Concern

WORLD'S HIGHEST HOTEL TO BE BUILT ON EVEREST

Climbers attempting Mount Everest may soon be able to contemplate the challenge ahead with a meal of pan-fried yak, washed down with goat's milk and a long soak in the bath. Planning permission has been granted for the world's highest hotel among the tents of the northern Base Camp on Everest's Tibetan side. The 52-bed hotel will be 'a flagship for green construction techniques' said the developer. Buddhists have blessed the site. There will be a bar and restaurant and dormitory-style chalets. Sensitive to environmentalist concerns, the hotel will run on solar power. Waste will also be recycled into energy. The scheme will cost £2.3 million and building should begin in April 2002. The hotel will charge around £70 a night. Target groups include budget tourists who can drive up to the hotel and enjoy the view from the restaurants as well as trekkers.

The scheme has appalled mountaineers and environmentalists who fear it will make the area around Everest a virtual theme park. 'I don't like the idea' said Bill Ruthven, honorary secretary of the Mount Everest Foundation. 'This is commercialising Everest. It should be left aloof from the masses.' Sir Chris Bonington, who led the first expedition up Everest's south-west face in 1975, called the plan regrettable but inevitable.

Environmental issues – building a hotel in the Himalayan mountains to the north of India **D**

Adapted from an article by Will Iredale in Sunday Times, 7 January 2001

---

2 Study **Source B**.
a Describe the scene in the photo.
b What is your view of this activity? Explain your view.
c Why do you think John McConnico took this photograph at the Pushkar Camel Fair?

3 Study **Source C**.
a List jobs being carried out by local people at the caves near Mumbai.
b What is your view of the behaviour of:
• tourists that create the jobs
• the local people?

c List advantages and disadvantages of creating international golf courses.
d On balance do you think they are good or bad for India and its people? Justify your view.

4 Study **Source D** and the photo on page 53.
a Describe the planned building development.
b In what ways will this development affect:
• the environment
• tourism to the area?
c Do you think this development should go ahead? Justify your view

4 Development through the Internet

Banking and financial institutions

African Development Bank

Asian Development Bank

Caribbean Development Bank

European Bank for Reconstruction and Development

International Bank for Reconstruction and Development

International Monetary Fund

The World Bank Group

Development networks

Eldis

EuForic - Europe's Forum on International Cooperation

Southbound - Third World Network

Third World Network (TWN)

Environment

GreenNet - Networking for the Environment, Peace and Human Rights

Rainforest Action Network

Two Way Track : Biodiversity Conservation and Ecotourism

Human rights

Human Rights Internet

Human Rights Web

Amnesty International
see NGOs - International

Multilateral organizations

AlertNet

ASEAN Secretariat

Development Association Committee

The Directorates - General and Services

International Labour Organization

OECD

World Food Programme

World Health Organization

UN Home Page

NGOs - International

Amnesty International

War Child

British Council

Charities Aid Foundation

Charity Net Site

Development NGO Links

Friends of the Earth

NGO Sites

One World

Oxfam

VSO

Government - UK

DFID Home Page

Foreign and Commonwealth Office

You have now completed the unit *People, Work and Development*. The DfID (*Department for International Development*) publishes a quarterly magazine about development in the world. Listed on this page are various organisations from the magazine that will help you research development issues. Visit www.heinemann.co.uk/hotlinks to find their websites

Choose *one* organization that interests you from the list. Find out what the organization you have chosen is doing about development issues in a *Less Economically Developed Country* (LEDC) of your choice.

Glossary

Term	Definition	Page
Adult literacy	The percentage of people over 16 years old in a country or region that can read and write	30
Arable	The type of farming that involves growing crops	40
The Brandt Report	A report produced in 1980 that divided the world into More Economically Developed Countries (MEDCs) and Less Economically Developed Countries (LEDCs)	16
Capitalism	An economic system in which the majority of goods and services are owned and managed by individuals and companies rather than by the state	22
City state	Large urban areas that have their own national government and are not ruled by other countries	48
Common Agricultural Policy (CAP)	Strategies for the control and development of farming that have been adopted by all member countries of the European Union	41
Communism	A system of government where most goods and services are owned and managed by the state and little private enterprise is allowed	22
Development agencies	These are created by the UK government to provide help in the form of grants, loans, ready-built factories and infrastructure to attract investment into areas of economic decline and high unemployment	46
Economic recession	A period of decline during which some industrial activity closes, people become unemployed and the negative multiplier operates	47
Economic recovery	A period during which economic activity rises from a period of economic recession, new employment opportunities are created and the positive multiplier operates	47
Entrêpot	A commercial port whose main function is to provide facilities for import and export and the collection and distribution of goods	48
European Economic Community (EEC)	A trading group of West European countries set up in 1958 following the success of the ECSC	20
European Union (EU)	The European Community – EC (formerly European Economic Community – EEC) has been known as the EU since a free-trade area was established within the member countries in 1993	20
European Coal and Steel Community (ECSC)	An agreement made in 1952 about trade in iron and steel between France, West Germany, Italy and Benelux (Belgium, Netherlands and Luxembourg). It led to the formation of the EEC	20
Favela	A Brazilian shanty town or squatter settlement	34
The First Industrial Nation	A term used to describe the UK as the first nation to change from an agricultural to an industrial economy during the eighteenth and nineteenth centuries	18
Formal employment	Official jobs with set hours and rates of pay. People who are formally employed pay direct taxes to the government	7
Free trade	The movement of goods and services within a country or trade group which does not require the payment of custom duties	33
Gender	Male or female	11
General Agreement on Trade and Tariffs (GATT)	An agreement between countries that encourages the removal of trade barriers to increase international trade and co-operation	33
Globalization	The expansion of a company from its original country to a position where it has branches in many countries. These have an important influence on world trade	32
Gross Domestic Product (GDP)	The total value of all the goods and services produced in a country in one year by all the people living in that country	23
Gross National Product (GNP)	The total value of all the goods and services produced by the people of a country in one year, whether or not they are living there at the time	22
Headloaders	Informal labourers, mostly women, who act as porters in the Indian textile industry. They are so-named because of the way they carry the materials	29
Independence	When a government takes on sole responsibility for making decisions about how to run the country it governs	19
Informal employment	Unofficial jobs that have no set hours or rates of pay. People who are informally employed may avoid paying tax and are usually self-employed	7
Infrastructure	The structure of communications and services required to support economic development e.g. power supplies, education, health, transport	52
Intermediate aid	Help usually given by organizations in MEDCs to people living in LEDCs. It often involves small-scale, labour-intensive schemes aimed at providing a sustainable future	34
International Monetary Fund (IMF)	The IMF was created in 1945. It is an international reserve of money held by the World Bank. It is used to strengthen trade links or for lending to countries in financial difficulties	34
Intis	The Peruvian unit of currency	17
Inward investment	Investment into a country usually from multi-national companies based in another country	44
Logistics	The organization of the distribution of goods and services	52
Multi-national companies	Large companies with a branch in more than one country. Decisions are made at a headquarters in one of those countries. They are also known as trans-national corporations (TNCs)	44

National Insurance Contributions — A system of compulsory deductions from pay from all adults below pensionable age and from employers in the UK. The money raised provides benefits such as social security, unemployment benefits and state pensions 10

Negative multiplier effect — A downward spiral of events that follow the decline of investment in a region such as decreased spending, the loss of other jobs and out-migration 47

Non-Government Organizations (NGO) — Groups of people who work with communities in order to improve their quality of life. They are separate from official local and national agencies but sometimes work with them. Most of their work is in LEDCs 32

Positive discrimination — A process whereby women, disabled people and others from minority groups are encouraged to take part in an activity or apply for a job 29

Positive multiplier effect — An upward spiral of events that follow a major investment in a region such as increased spending, the creation of other jobs and in-migration 47

Protectionism — Where the government of a country uses policies that prevent or discourage the import of foreign goods. This enables its own producers to benefit from the lack of foreign competition 32

Quality of life — The happiness, well-being and satisfaction of a person. Among the many factors that influence quality of life are the person's family, income and access to services 9

Quota — A numerical limit on immigrants or on imports 32

Referendum — The process whereby an elected government chooses to ask the electorate to make a direct decision by voting on a specific issue 20

Rugmark — An NGO that encourages the production and sale of rugs and carpets that have not used child labour 31

Self-employed — Where a person chooses to work for her/himself as a paid employee and accepts responsibility for paying deductions such as taxes to the government 7

Self-sufficient — A situation where a person or a community provides all its basic needs without having to trade with groups outside that community 20

Smelting — The extraction of a metal from its ore by melting 54

Source — In this case, the money that is taken out of a person's gross pay before they receive it. It includes such deductions as income tax, national insurance and contributions to a pension fund. The person is left with their net disposable income 7

Standard of living — Those factors which affect a person's quality of life and which can be measured. Many measures of a person's standard of living are to do with possessions 9

Tariff barrier — Custom duties payable on imports. They are used to raise the price of imports so that home producers can compete effectively 32

Technical Assistance to the CIS (TACIS) — Help in the form of technical expertise from the EU to countries of the former CIS to improve and develop their infrastructures 42

Tiger economies — Newly-industrialised countries (NICs) in South-east Asia that showed rapid economic growth in the late twentieth century largely through the creation and expansion of multi-national companies, e.g. LG from South Korea 32

Traditional aid — Help usually given by organizations in MEDCs to people living in LEDCs. It often involves the lending of large sums of money to develop capital intensive schemes such as multi-purpose dams 34

United Nations Development Programme (UNDP) — The United Nations is a group of 185 nations originally formed after the Second World War (1939-1945). It is committed to a development programme that includes the sustainable development of the world and its human potential. It also encourages equality, and the elimination of poverty 36

World Bank — An organization set up by MEDCs who contribute funds that can be used for lending money for development projects in LEDCs 34

World Trade Organization — A group set up to oversee the international trading system agreed by GATT in 1994. It is run by representatives of the governments of its member countries 33